**GOLDEN HART GUIDES**

# *Yorkshire*

## *York, Yorkshire Dales & North York Moors*

Ian Thackrah

**SIDGWICK & JACKSON LONDON**
in association with Trusthouse Forte

914·28

Front cover photo: York Minster
Back cover photo: Burnsall

Photographs by the British Tourist
Authority, with the exception of
ps 7, 9, 11, 12 (Mansell Collection)
and ps 4/5, 14, 47 (bottom), 50 (top), 51
(J. I. Thackrah)

Compiled and designed by Paul Watkins
Additional material by Richard Thackrah
Editorial associate: Jo Darke
Maps: John Flower

First published in Great Britain 1985
by Sidgwick and Jackson in association
with Trusthouse Forte

ISBN 0-283-99203-4

Photoset by Tellgate Ltd, London WC1
Printed and bound in Great Britain
By Hazell Watson & Viney Limited,
Aylesbury, Bucks
for Sidgwick & Jackson Limited,
1 Tavistock Chambers, Bloomsbury Way,
London WC1A 2SG

*Contents*

4 **Introduction**

7 **Yorkshire**
A Brief History

14 **The Best of the Region**
excluding City of York

26 **York**

32 York Map

40 **Gazetteer**

95 **Index**

96 **Regional Map**

# Introduction

*West Tanfield in Wensleydale*

North Yorkshire is the largest county in England, with an area of 3211 square miles but a population of only 666,610. Its boundaries enclose the Yorkshire Dales and North York Moors National Parks, the rich agricultural lands of the Vales of Mowbray and Pickering and the Plain of York, and a fine coastal area stretching from Staithes to Filey. Just south of Filey are the magnificent Bempton Cliffs and Flamborough Head and the resort of Bridlington, all in Humberside.

Fortunately for the visitor the region is hardly touched by the industry on its northern and southern borders. The area is still largely rural, with vast open spaces that belie the image of England as a small, overcrowded country. The green dales and rolling moorlands can be enjoyed even more with the knowledge that so much of it is National Park or National Trust land.

In the Dales Park area there are five principal dales – Swaledale, Wensleydale, Nidderdale, Wharfedale and Airedale. With the exception of Wensleydale, named after its principal village, all take their names from the rivers flowing through them, and all offer a wide range of scenery to be enjoyed not only in the dales themselves but in the many side valleys or minor dales.

All five rivers flow past attractive villages and towns which provide a wide range of accommodation and facilities for the visitor and many features of interest in their locality. Easily accessible from the major roads, the dales possess outstanding beauty spots

and places of architectural and historical interest. Swaledale has Richmond with its castle and Georgian Theatre; Wensleydale the beauty of Aysgarth Falls and the magnificence of Fountains Abbey; Nidderdale the eccentricities of nature represented by Stump Cross Caverns and Brimham Rocks; Wharfedale the delightful town of Ilkley and superb Harewood House; and Airedale/Malhamdale the wildness of Malham Cove and Tarn, and Gordale Scar.

The Moors Park is quite different. Bounded roughly by the A19, A170, A171, A172 and A173, it is crossed by only one major road, the A169. There are many minor roads, mostly narrow and winding, and many with steep gradients. Most of them run in a north-south direction following the valleys which cut deeply into the high, wild and remote moorland of bracken, heather, peat bogs and forests. The few villages, and the small market towns such as Guisborough, Stokesley, Thirsk, Helmsley, Kirkbymoorside and Pickering are all on the periphery, spread out along the major roads. Of the villages the most frequented are Goathland, Hutton-le-Hole and Thornton Dale, but there are many alternatives to this popular trio. Rivers are short and apart from the Esk, might be more properly described as becks or streams. Geological features of particular interest are the Bridestones, the Hole of Horcum and Newton Dale. The vast tracts of forest with their picnic areas, way-marked routes, and diversity of animals and bird life offer a special appeal to walkers and naturalists.

Separating the Parks are the Howardian Hills, Plain of York and Vale of Pickering. These are for the most part devoted to agriculture, the small towns serving as marketing centres with a little light industry. In this central area is the city of York and the town of Harrogate, which make fine bases for exploring the region.

The coastal towns, particularly Scarborough, offer a full range of entertainment and amenities. Quieter places are the small coastal villages catering for holiday-makers, such as Staithes, Runswick Bay and Robin Hood's Bay. Like Scarborough and Whitby these smaller places have splendid cliff scenery, attractive bays and fishing harbours and a bracing atmosphere.

The attractions of North Yorkshire's coast are complementary to the glorious hinterland of hills, moors, valleys, forests and rivers and the splendid man-made heritage of its country houses, gardens and parks, abbeys, castles and museums. Among the stately homes, Castle Howard is recognised as one of the finest in England, and Rievaulx Abbey a splendid monument to the glories of pre-Reformation architecture. Among the museums the Captain Cook Museums at Middlesbrough and Great Ayton, and Hutton-le-Hole Folk Museum are outstanding examples of their kind. Above all there is incomparable York, with its magnificent Minster, beautiful churches, superb Castle Museum, and elegant streets with their finely restored Georgian and Victorian shop-fronts.

The region offers a wide range of activities, from freshwater and sea fishing to climbing and pot-holing; from riding to golf, and from gliding to sailing. The moors and dales are ideal for walking, and for the study of botany, geology and ornithology. Railway enthusiasts will enjoy the North Yorkshire Moors Railway, running from Pickering to Grosmont.

For those who enjoy tracking down the haunts of the famous, the region provides many possibilities. These include Otley and Harewood with their Thomas Chippendale associations; Great Ayton, Staithes and Whitby with their Captain Cook connections; Coxwold with memories of Oliver Cromwell and Laurence Sterne; and Scarborough with its family home of the Sitwells.

Details of Yorkshire's many attractions and activities will be found in 'The Best of the Region' section of the book, together with a selection of walks and motoring tours. The Gazetteer provides a summary of the principal places of interest in the county, and special coverage, with a walking tour, is given to York.

# Yorkshire

## A Brief History

Byland Abbey

**Prehistory** The earliest inhabitants of the region were hunter/fishers, a group settling near the coast at Starr Carr, south of Scarborough, *c.* 10,000BC. Sea level varied considerably during this late glacial and early Mesolithic period, and settlements were gradually moved to higher ground, where pygmy flints and carved bone harpoons have been discovered. In beach deposits covered by glacial debris, remains of many animals have been found: the bones of sub-tropical species discovered in a cave in Kirk Dale, near Kirkbymoorside, show that the climate was at one time much warmer.

Around 2000BC a new group of settlers known by their form of building – Megalithic – appeared in the country. They built colossal stone structures: long barrows, standing stones and stone circles, many of which are now well-known monuments, such as the Devil's Arrows at Boroughbridge and the 'cup and ring' stones on Rombalds Moor, Ilkley. Other monuments from this period are the henges, which took the form of circular areas 60 to 600ft in diameter surrounded by ditches with high banks. The largest are found north and east of Ripon.

From 1800-1500BC there was a migration from the Continent into Britain of the Beaker Folk, who entered the country by the Humber and spread over the Wolds, crossing into north-west Yorkshire via the York moraine. Bronze was used to make knives and daggers, wheat was cultivated and settlements took the form of small farmsteads.

The Middle Bronze Age was a time when the 'native' people, descendants of Mesolithic and

Neolithic stocks, mingled with the Beaker folk and absorbed them. They buried their dead in small circular barrows, found all over the area. The Late Bronze Age saw the immigration of other groups, most importantly the Hallstatt people from the northern Alps (*c.* 500BC), who brought their Iron Age culture to England (settlement on Scarborough Castle Hill).

In the Iron Age, most settlements were built on land that was well drained and free of forest cover. The limestone country has revealed abundant remains of this period, most numerous settlement types being a single hut with one or more irregular enclosures. A later group from Europe, the Parisii, appeared in the 3rd century BC. A warrior tribe from the Marne-Seine area in northern France, they were noted for their love of horses and chariots, which were often buried with them. Remains have been found near Skipton and Ripon and in upper Wensleydale. These martial invaders conquered the native Brigantes, who though initially subdued were to become a strong tribal confederacy by the 1st century AD.

**The Romans** Soon after the Roman invasion the attack on the North began, culminating in the Pennines in the Battle of Stanwick (74AD). This resulted in the bulk of the native Brigantes retreating into the western dales, and commenced the Romano-British period of Yorkshire's history. The most notable Roman innovation was the development of agriculture based upon arable fields. These ancient fields can still be seen from the air in some parts of the Dales.

The Romans chose the larger Brigantian villages, with which they had some trade, for their forts. These included Cataractonium (Catterick); Isurium (Aldborough); Olicana (Ilkley) and Eboracum (York). The Brigantes were ruled by a king or queen, and had a gold coinage which they used for trading. Outside the towns, the people lived either in small villages, farmsteads or even in single huts with one or two fields and small enclosures for sheep and cattle. They suffered harsh conditions, living in great poverty and having to endure a cold, wet climate. The Brigantes were more warlike than the neighbouring tribe, the Parisii, who were predominant in eastern Yorkshire.

The most strategically situated of the Roman camps was Eboracum (York). Founded in 71AD, it was located on a glacial moraine on the navigable Ouse and Foss rivers, within easy reach of the Wolds on one side and the Aire-Ribble Gap (the lowest of the Pennine Passes) on the other. Derventio (Malton), was founded at a similar time on the edge of a corn-growing area from which bases could be established against the hostile tribesmen of the moors.

Most inhabitants of Roman Britain obtained their living from the land. There were two kinds of farmers: the villa owners and the peasants. Interspersed with the villa estates, composed of comfortable centrally-heated houses on good lowland, were the small-holdings or sheep runs of the un-Romanized peasants on the poorer highland. The road system, a vital element in the conduct of trade and warfare, was based on York.

**Saxons, Danes and Vikings** The departure of the Romans in 410AD was followed by the Anglo-Saxon invasions of the mid-5th century. The native Britons were either absorbed by the new settlers or forced westwards. Four Saxon kingdoms were created, the northernmost running from the Humber to Hadrian's Wall, known as Northumbria.

The Saxons knew how to use metal, and were proficient in weaving and pottery and building in wood, clearing large areas of forest for this purpose. In Saxon society, loyalty to the thane or king was a matter of honour and self-respect. A record of this may be seen today on Fylingdales Moor: a Bronze Age barrow with a stone cross marking the burial spot of Lilla, thane of Edwin of Northumbria, who died protecting his king from an assassin.

*St Paulinus: York Minster window*

A major event in Anglo-Saxon history was the conversion of the English to Christianity. In the North, this task was undertaken by one of St Augustine's monks, Paulinus. The pagan King Edwin was converted by Paulinus and baptised in a wooden church on the site of the future York Minister (627AD).

This event marked the foundation of the Roman church in York with Paulinus as its bishop (and later archbishop).

With the establishment of the Celtic (Irish) mission at Lindisfarne in present-day Northumberland, the Celtic Church exerted increasing influence on Northumbria, the missionaries pushing further south into the other Saxon kingdoms. The confrontation between the two churches had ultimately to be resolved, and in 664, at Whitby, an important synod was called by King Oswy of Northumbria which resulted in the pre-eminence of a strongly organized and authoritarian Roman church.

The conversion of the English in Yorkshire was commemorated by the erection of crosses on the moors, some of which are still standing.

By the late 8th century raiders from Denmark and Norway began to descend on the English coast, attacks which were to culminate in the great Danish invasion of 865. While the Danes were fighting in England and making settlements, Vikings made their incursions in the north. Travelling either from the east coast via the River Ouse, or from the west via the Aire-Ribble Gap, they reached York, where they established an independent Norse kingdom.

The history of the region from this time until the Norman Conquest is confused, with York subjected to a variety of rulers – Norse, Irish and Northumbrian – who were often independent of the Saxon or Danish kings of England. It was in this period that the region achieved its essentially Scandinavian character. The Danes settled all over the north-east of England, most intensively in Yorkshire, becoming the ancestors of modern Yorkshiremen. The word 'Yorkshire' was first recorded in 1055, but the area so designated was probably marked out 200 years earlier. This was the Viking Halfdan's settlement, corresponding roughly to the traditional county and later divided by the Danes into the three parts known as the North, West and East Ridings (from the Danish word *thriding* or third part).

York meanwhile progressed from a small centre of royal and ecclesiastical administration to a thriving town whose population was second only to that of London.

**The Normans** With their common ancestry, the Normans were continuing the tradition of the Nordic invasions of the Danes and Vikings when they landed on the Sussex coast in 1066. A factor contributing to William's success was, in fact, the simultaneous invasion of the Vikings under Harald Hardrada, which had diverted the Saxon army of Harold of England to the North. At Stamford Bridge, east of York, Harold had decisively defeated the Norse king, but the battle exhausted the English and three weeks later, after the return march south, they were overwhelmed by the Normans at Hastings.

Many Norman families, such as the Percys and the Nevilles, obtained lands in Yorkshire. In all there were about 40 castles built in the county, including the two royal ones at York. The position of the countrymen changed for the worse, the free landowners decreasing in numbers as they were reduced to the level of serfs or villeins, compelled to work for all or part of the week on their lords' lands.

The rebellions that resulted from this oppression were put down savagely by the Normans, who laid the country waste and put the inhabitants to the sword. It took years for the region to recover, but Yorkshire's geographical position ensured that it continued to be the stage on which much of the drama of England's national history would be played. Remote from the capital, it was still accessible to it by virtue of the flat country between York and London, and the Roman road – Ermine Street. Dissident barons or pretenders to the throne could use Yorkshire as a base for organizing rebellions. Before the news could reach London they were able to march south and try their luck against the king. He for his part might march north, and seek out his enemies in their own lands. Yorkshire was also a frontier zone open to attacks by the Scots, but from which English counter-attacks could be mounted, as at the Battle of Northallerton in 1138. To ward off incursions many of the towns were encircled by walls. York's circuit of 4840 yards enclosed 263 acres.

Despite its harshness, the benefits of Norman rule were considerable. The Normans prevented any further invasions from abroad

*Fountains Abbey: an early 19th-century engraving*

and imposed a degree of law and order on the countryside. Many of their castles (Scarborough, Skipton, Richmond) have survived as impressive monuments and their skill as builders can be seen in the great ecclesiastical buildings of the period (York Minster, Fountains and Rievaulx Abbeys).

**The Tudors** Although many of the battles of the Wars of the Roses (1455-85) were fought in Yorkshire, the Yorkists' association was with the royal house of York, rather than with the county. The root cause of the later hostility of Yorkshire to the Tudors was Henry VII's new style of government, the keynote of which was sovereignty. In place of the feudal overlords with absolute power over their vassals, there was a king who had the ultimate authority over all his subjects. In 1487 the defeated Yorkists led by Lambert Simnel, a pretender to the throne, tried to oust Henry, but after failure to capture York the rebellion collapsed.

Another rebellion began in Yorkshire after Henry VIII became head of the Church of England and dissolved the monasteries. Led by Robert Aske, with the support of many county families – Scrope, Neville, Constable, Fairfax, Norton and Percy – this rising, 'The Pilgrimage of Grace' also failed. However, the point was made that the North was Roman Catholic and prepared to fight to remain so; and there was a resentment at the growing power of central government and a conviction that the North was receiving less than its due.

During the Catholic reformation of Mary Tudor, persecution was on a small scale in Yorkshire, as Protestants were few in number. In the reign of Elizabeth I, when Mary, Queen of Scots became the focus for Catholic plots, there was a rising of the Northern Earls, but with the capture of Mary the revolt collapsed. For a brief period, at the start of her long years of imprisonment in England, Mary was held in Bolton Castle (1568/9).

**The Civil War** With the development of the weaving industry and the increased profits of the trade of its east coast ports, Yorkshire's prosperity increased in the 16th and 17th centuries. At the start of the Civil War Charles I chose York, England's second city, as his seat of government. The city was Royalist in outlook, as were the majority of the county families of North and East Yorkshire. The rest of the county was, however, pro-Parliament, with support for Cromwell in the West Riding, the major seaport of Hull and the castle and town of Scarborough. With the county so divided, the local gentry were fighting purely local campaigns, with forces that they had raised themselves, against fellow Yorkshiremen on the opposite side. After the Parliamentary victory at Marston Moor (1644) and the surrender of York, the king lost command of the North.

16 years later York played its part in the Restoration when General Monk, commander of the Commonwealth army in Scotland, arrived in the city to receive the summons from the House of Commons (the Rump) to come to London to restore order in the capital during the pro-Royalist disturbances. Monk's subsequent declaration for a free Parliament ensured the eventual recall of Charles II.

**Age of elegance** In 18th-century Yorkshire the aristocracy held sway, favoured by the inequity of the electoral representation. There were few boroughs in the North: those in the area included York, Ripon, Boroughbridge, Knaresborough, Richmond, Thirsk, Northallerton, Malton and Scarborough. In the country, votes were given to those owning land on which they paid 40 shillings a year in rates. The franchise was thus

confined to the gentry and a few yeoman farmers, and excluded all tenant farmers and labourers.

With their great estates, the privileged classes began to make their mark on the landscape, recruiting the best architects and landscape designers to build and decorate their country houses. The patronage of the playwright, and untried architect, John Vanbrugh, by Charles Howard, Earl of Carlisle, resulted in the magnificent Castle Howard.

In an age of elegance, lawlessness and violence were endemic. A popular crime – highway robbery – was linked to the increased amount of travel on improved roads; the exploits of Dick Turpin being particularly well known. Smuggling was also rife along the isolated coves of the east coast. Legitimate trade was however carried on by the ports – Captain Cook's earliest sea experiences being on London-bound colliers. Woollens were exported and whaling was a profitable activity.

**The Industrial Revolution** In the mid-18th century most of the population of Britain lived in the country and made its living from farming. A century later most people were city-dwellers, working in industry. In Yorkshire the availability of raw materials and water power brought particularly dramatic changes. Most industrial activity was concentrated in the west and south of the county, but the labour for the new factories was recruited from the country areas and there was a decisive shift of population to the towns.

To cater for the growth in industry, there were rapid improvements in transport. Canals were constructed, and turnpike trusts set up to build new roads. With the invention of the railway, however, road construction was soon outstripped by the rail lines. York became an early railway centre, within easy reach of industry on the Tees and in the West Riding, and resorts on the Yorkshire coast, as well as being a halfway stage between London and Edinburgh. When the first train ran from York to Scarborough in 1845, free beer was laid on at Castle Howard, bells were rung, and at Scarborough the mayor and corporation led the entire body of citizens to meet the train at the station.

Parliamentary reform, with a fairer system of representation, brought social changes that improved the quality of life for the people of Yorkshire. The drudgery of life in the mills and factories was alleviated by more humane working conditions, and with increased leisure activity the people were able to make more of the pleasures of the Dales and Moors and the Yorkshire coast. With the advance of tourism in the 20th century, the tendency towards an appreciation of the countryside and the conservation of its beauties has continued.

**Boundary changes** In 1974 the boundaries of Yorkshire were redrawn, parts of it being absorbed by Lancashire and Durham and the new counties of Cumbria, Cleveland and Humberside. The remainder of the county was divided between the administrative units of North Yorkshire, which includes most of the old North Riding; West Yorkshire, containing most of the old West Riding, and South Yorkshire.

*Castle Howard: an early 19th-century engraving*

# The Best of the Region

excluding City of York (p.26)

**A summary of the places of interest in the region, with opening times. The location, with map reference, and description of each place, is shown in the Gazetteer. Names in bold are Gazetteer entries, and those with an \*asterisk are considered to be of outstanding interest. (NT) indicates properties owned by the National Trust**

*The Strid, River Wharfe*

## Places of Interest

### Churches

Those listed are specially worth a visit, either for the building itself or for a particular feature such as brasses, heraldry, tombs or wall paintings.

**\*Ampleforth Abbey** St Laurence

**Aysgarth** St Andrew

**\*Bedale** St Gregory

**\*Bolton Abbey** Priory Church

**Bolton-on-Swale** St Mary

**\*Bridlington** St Mary

**Coxwold** St Michael

**\*Easby Abbey** St Agatha

**\*Egton Bridge** St Hedda

**\*Fountains Abbey** (Studley Royal) St Mary the Virgin

**\*Helmsley** All Saints

**Hubberholme** St Michael & All Angels

**Ilkley** All Saints

**Kirkby Malham** St Michael the Archangel

**Kirkbymoorside** All Saints, (Kirk Dale) St Gregory's Minster

**\*Lastingham** St Mary

**Malton** St Mary, St Michael

**Newby Hall** (Skelton) Christ the Consoler

**\*Nun Monkton** St Mary

**Otley** All Saints

**\*Pickering** St Peter & St Paul

**Richmond** St Mary

**Ripley** All Saints

**\*Ripon** Cathedral of St Peter & St Wilfrid

**\*Skipton** Holy Trinity

**\*Snape** St Mary

**Thirsk** St Mary

**Topcliffe** St Columba

**West Tanfield** St Nicholas

**\*Whitby** St Mary

**YORK** see p. 26

## Historic Houses

Admission to most historic houses is between £1-2 (children half-price).

**Bedale** Bedale Hall
Easter-Sep, Tue 9-5

**Beningbrough Hall** (NT)
Apr-Oct, Tue-Thur, Sat, Sun & Bank Hol Mons 12-6. Closed Good Fri

**Bolton-on-Swale** Kiplin Hall
End May-Aug, Sun, Wed & Bank Hols 2-5

**Bridlington** Sewerby Hall
See *Museums, Art Galleries & Visitor Centres*

**\*Burton Agnes Hall**
Mid Apr-Oct, daily 11-5

**\*Castle Howard**
End Mar-Oct, daily. House, cafeteria & costume galleries 11.30-5; Grounds 10.30-5

**Coxwold** Newburgh Priory
Mid May-Aug, Wed 2-6

**Coxwold** Shandy Hall
Jun-Sep, Wed 2-6; also
Jul-Sep Sun, 2.30-4.30

**Gilling East** Gilling Castle
(Hall & Great Chamber)
Mon-Fri 10-12 & 2-4;
Garden daily

**\*Harewood House**
Apr-Oct, daily from 11 am;
Nov, Feb & Mar, Sun only.
Grounds open from 10am.
Closing time varies with
season.

**Hovingham** Hovingham
Hall
Early May-mid Sep.
Tue-Thur 11-7 (parties of 15
or more only, by
arrangement)

**Leyburn** Constable Burton
Hall
House: Sat, Sun & Bank Hol
Mons 1-5
Gardens: daily 9-6.30

**\*Newby Hall**
Apr-Sep, Tue-Sun & Bank
Hol Mons 1-5.30 (last
admission 5); Grounds from
11

**Nunnington Hall** (NT)
Apr-Oct, Tue-Thur, Sat &
Sun 2-6; Bank Hol Mons
11-6. Closed Good Fri

**\*Ripley** Ripley Castle
Apr & May, Sat & Sun;
Jun-Sep, Tue-Thur, Sat &
Sun 2-6; Easter-Aug Bank
Hols, 11-6; Garden
Apr-Sep, daily 11-6

**Ripon** Markenfield Hall
Apr-Oct, Mon 10-12.30 &
2.15-5; May, Tue-Sun,
grounds only

**Ripon** Norton Conyers
Jun-early Sep, Sun & Bank
Hols 2-5.30; Garden open
daily

**Skipton** Broughton Hall
Bank Hols 11-5, or by
arrangement (parties of 15
or more)

**\*Sledmere House**
Bank Hol Mons; Easter, and
following Suns to end May;
Jun-Sep, Tue-Thur, Sat &
Sun; 1.30-5.30

**Thirsk** Osgodby Hall
Easter-Sep, Sat, Sun &
Bank Hols 2-5

**YORK** see p. 26

# Parks, Gardens & Wildlife

(See also *Nature Reserves*,
p. 18)

Admission to the gardens of
historic houses is usually
included in a combined
ticket for house and garden.
(See admission to Historic
Houses above.) Where the
garden can be visited
separately this is usually
about half the price of the
combined ticket. The
entrance fee for other
gardens open to the public is
usually in the range 30-50p
(children half-price or less).

**Appletreewick** Parceval
Hall Garden
Easter-Oct, 10-6

**Beningbrough Hall**
House & garden
See *Historic Houses*

**Bolton-on-Swale** Kiplin
Hall
House & garden
See *Historic Houses*

**Bridlington** Sewerby Hall
Park & Zoo
10-dusk

**\*Castle Howard**
House, gardens & park
See *Historic Houses*

**Coxwold** Newburgh Priory
House & garden
See *Historic Houses*

**Coxwold** Shandy Hall
House & garden
See *Historic Houses*

**\*Fountains Abbey** &
Studley Royal Park
Abbey ruin & parkland
See *Castles, Ruins,
Monuments & Ancient Sites*

**Gilling East** Gilling Castle
House & garden
See *Historic Houses*

**Harewood House**
House, bird garden &
adventure playground
See *Historic Houses*

**\*Harrogate** Harlow Car
Gardens, Valley Gardens
Daily 9-7.30 or dusk

**Helmsley** Duncombe Park
May-Aug, Wed 10-4
(Admission from Estate
Office)

**Hovingham** Hovingham
Hall
House & garden
See *Historic Houses*

**Kilnsey** Kilnsey Park &
Trout Farm
Daily 9.30-5

**Knaresborough**
Conyngham Hall Zoo
Easter-Oct, daily from 10

**Leyburn** Constable Burton
Hall Garden
See *Historic Houses*

**Newby Hall**
House & garden
See *Historic Houses*

**Nunnington Hall**
See *Historic Houses*

**Pickering** Flamingoland
Leisure Park
Apr-Sep, 10-dusk

**\*Rievaulx Terrace &
Temples** (NT)
Apr-Oct, daily 10.30-6, last
admission 5.30 (Ionic
Temple closed 1-2) Closed
Good Fri

**Ripley** Ripley Castle
House & garden
See *Historic Houses*

**Ripon** Lightwater Valley
Leisure Centre
Easter Hol, Jun-Aug &
Bank Hols daily; Apr, May
& Sep, Sat & Sun 10.30-dusk

**Ripon** Norton Conyers
House and garden
See *Historic Houses*

**Sandsend** Mulgrave Woods
Jun-Apr, Sat, Sun & Wed

**Scarborough** Peasholm
Park
Public pleasure gardens

**Scarborough** Zoo &
Marineland
Easter-Sep, daily 10-8

**Skipton** Broughton Hall
House & garden
See *Historic Houses*

**Sledmere House**
House & garden
See *Historic Houses*

**Snape** Thorp Perrow
Arboretum
Apr-Oct, dawn-dusk

**Thornton Dale** Low
Dalby Forest Visitor Centre
See *Museums, Galleries &
Visitor Centres*

**Whitby** Pannett Park
Public gardens

**YORK** see p. 27

## Castles, Ruins, Monuments & Ancient Sites

Unless otherwise stated,
these sites are accessible at
all reasonable times

**Barden Tower**
Ruined 15th-c. hunting
lodge

**\*Bolton Abbey** Bolton Priory
12th-c. priory ruin

**Bolton Abbey** Cavendish
Memorial
Memorial to Lord Frederick
Cavendish

**Bolton Castle**
14th-c. castle
Tue-Sun, 10-5

**Boroughbridge** Devil's
Arrows
Bronze Age monument

**Burton Agnes Hall**
(Rudston) Rudston
Monolith
Prehistoric standing stone

**Byland Abbey**
12th-c. abbey ruin
Mar 15-Oct 15, Mon-Sat
9.30-6.30, Sun 2-6.30; Oct
16-Mar 14, Mon-Sat 9.30-4,
Sun 2-4 (not Dec 24-26, Jan
1 & 1st Mon in May)

**Castleton** Ralph Cross, Fat
Betty
Wayfarers' crosses

**Catterick Bridge** Castle Hill
Norman motte and bailey
remains

**Cawthorn Roman Camps**
Roman site

**Cawthorn Roman Camps**
Wade's Causeway
Roman road

**\*Easby Abbey**
12th-c. abbey ruin
Times as for Byland Abbey

**Flamborough Head** Danes'
Dyke
Brigantian fortification

**\*Fountains Abbey** (NT)
12th-c. abbey ruin
Apr-Sep, daily 10-7
(Jul-Aug closed at 8);
Oct-Mar, daily 10-4 (closed
Dec 24-25). Floodlit
opening Apr-Sep, Fri & Sat
until 11

**Gilling East** Gilling Castle
14th-18th-c. fortified
mansion
See *Historic Houses*

**Goathland** Lilla Howe
Medieval wayfarers' cross
and grave monument

**Grinton** Maiden Castle
Romano-British site

**Guisborough** Priory
12th-c. priory ruin
Times as for Byland Abbey

**Helmsley** Castle
12th-c. castle ruin
Times as for Byland Abbey

**Ilkley** Swastika Stone
Iron Age incised stone

**Jervaulx Abbey**
12th-c. abbey ruin

**Kilburn** White Horse
Chalk figure cut into hillside

**Kirkham Priory**
12th-c. priory ruin
Times as for Byland Abbey

**Knaresborough** Castle
Norman castle ruin
End May-Sep, Mon-Fri
10-5, Sun 11-5

**Marston Moor** Obelisk
Battle Monument

**\*Middleham** Castle
11th-c. castle ruin
Times as for Byland Abbey

**\*Osmotherley** Mount Grace
Priory (NT)
14th-c. priory ruin
Times as for Byland Abbey

**Pateley Bridge** Yorke's
Folly
Mock ruined tower

**Pickering** Castle
12th-c. castle ruin
Times as for Byland Abbey

**Reeth** Ellerton Priory
15th-c. nunnery ruin

**Reeth** Marrick Priory
Benedictine nunnery ruin

**\*Richmond** Castle
Norman castle ruin
Times as for Byland Abbey

**\*Rievaulx Abbey**
12th-c. abbey ruin
Times as for Byland Abbey

**Ripley** Ripley Castle
Tudor castle
See *Historic Houses*

**Scarborough** Castle
12th-c. castle ruin
Times as for Byland Abbey

**Settle** Victoria Cave
Prehistoric cave

**Sheriff Hutton** Castle
14th-c. castle ruin

**Skipton** Castle
14th-17th-c. castle remains
Mon-Sat 10-7, Sun 2-7 or
sunset

**Topcliffe** Maiden Bower
Motte and bailey earthworks

**Whitby** Whitby Abbey
11th-c. abbey ruin
Times as for Byland Abbey

**YORK** see p. 26

## Museums, Galleries & Visitor Centres

**Aldborough** Roman Museum
Apr-Sep, Mon-Sat
9.30-6.30, Sun 2-6.30

**Aysgarth** Yorkshire
Museum of Carriages &
Horse Drawn Vehicles
End Apr-mid Oct, daily
11.30-5.30

**Bedale** Bedale Hall
Georgian mansion & craft
museum
See *Historic Houses*

**Bolton Castle** Dales
Museum
See *Historic Houses*

**Bridlington** Bayle Gate
Museum
Jun-Sep, Tue-Fri 11-4; also
Tue & Thur 7-9

**Bridlington** Harbour &
History Museum
Apr-Sep, daily 10-5.30
(Jul-Aug 10-9)

**Bridlington** Sewerby Hall
Art Gallery & Museum
Easter-Sep, Sun-Fri
10-12.30 & 1.30-6, Sat
1.30-6

**\*Castle Howard** Costume
Galleries
See *Historic Houses*

**Danby** Moors Centre
Easter-Oct, daily 10-5;
Nov-Easter, Sun 12-4

**Filey** Folk Museum
End May-early Sep, Sun-Fri
2-5

**Grassington** Upper
Wharfedale Museum
Apr-Oct, daily 2-4.30;
Nov-Mar, Sat & Sun 2-4.30

**Great Ayton** Captain Cook
Schoolroom Museum
Easter-Oct, daily 2-4.30

**\*Great Ayton** (Marton)
Captain Cook Birthplace
Museum
Summer 10-6, winter 10-4

**Harrogate** Art Gallery
Mon-Fri 10-5, Sat 10-4

**Harrogate** Royal Pump
Room Museum
Mon-Sat 10.30-5, Sun 2-5;
Oct-Mar 10.30-4

**Hawes** Upper Dales Folk
Museum
Apr-Sep, Mon-Sat 11-1 &
2-5, Sun 2-5

**\*Hutton-le-Hole** Ryedale
Folk Museum
End Mar-Oct, daily 11-6

**Ilkley** Manor House
Museum & Art Gallery
Apr-Sep, Tue-Sun & Bank
Hol Mons 10-6; Oct-Mar,
Tue-Sun 10-5

**Ilkley** White Wells
Easter-mid Oct, Sat, Sun &
Bank Hol Mons 2-6

**Knaresborough** Old Court
House Museum
Easter-Sep, Mon-Sat 10-5,
Sun 11-5; Oct-Easter, Sun
only 1.30-4.30

**Leyburn** Chandler Gallery
Mon-Sat 9.30-5 (Wed
9.30-1); Jun-Sep, also Sun
11-4

**Malton** Museum
May-Sep, Mon-Sat 10-4,
Sun 2-4; Oct-Apr Sat only
1-3 (closed Dec)

**Otley** Museum
Mon, Tue & Fri 10-12.30

**Pateley Bridge** Nidderdale
Museum
Easter-May, Sat & Sun;
Jun-Sep daily; Oct-Easter,
Sun 2-5

**\*Pickering** Beck Isle
Museum of Rural Life
Apr-Oct, daily 10.30-12.30
& 2-5 (August until 7)

**Pickering** North Yorkshire
Moors Railway Information
Centre
Apr-Oct (Time-table from
Pickering Station)

**Reeth** Swaledale Folk
Museum
Easter-Oct, daily 10.30-6

**\*Richmond** Georgian
Theatre & Museum
Easter & May-Sep, daily
2.30-5 (Sat & Bank Hol
Mons, 10.30-1)

**Richmond** Green Howards
Museum
Apr-Oct, Mon-Sat 9.30-4.30
Sun 2-4.30; Nov-Mar,
Mon-Fri 9.30-4.30

**Richmond** Richmondshire
Museum
Jun-Sep, daily 2-5

**Ripon** Prison & Police
Museum
May-mid Sep, Tue-Sat &
Bank Hol Mons 1-4

**Ripon** Wakeman's House
Museum
Apr-Sep, Mon-Sat 10-5,
Sun 2-5

**Scarborough** Crescent Art
Gallery
Tue-Sat, 10-1 & 2-5;
Jun-Sep, also Sun 2-5

**Scarborough** Rotunda
Archaeological Museum
Tue-Sat, 10-1 & 2-5;
Jun-Sep, also Sun 2-5

**Scarborough** Wood End
Natural History Museum
Tue-Sat, 10-1 & 2-5;
May-Sep, also Sun 2-5

**Settle** Museum of North
Craven Life
May & Jun, Sat & Sun;
Jul-Sep, Tue-Sun; Oct-Apr,
Sat; 2-5

**Skipton** Craven Museum
Apr-Sep, Mon-Fri 10-5, Sat
10-5 with lunch break, Sun
2-5; Oct-Mar, Mon-Fri 2-5,
Sat 2-4.30

**\*Skipton** (Haworth) Brontë
Parsonage
Daily Apr-Sep, 11-5.30;
Oct-Mar 11-4.30

**Skipton** George Leatt
Industrial & Folk Museum
Spring & summer, Wed &
Fri from 2, Sat & Sun from 12

**Stump Cross Caverns**
Caves & Visitor Centre
Easter-Sep, daily

**Thirsk** Museum
May-Sep, Mon-Sat 11-5,
Sun 2.30-5

**Thornton Dale** Low Dalby
Forest Visitor Centre &
Wildlife Museum
Apr-Sep daily, 11-5

**Whitby** Lifeboat Museum
Jun-Sep, Mon-Sat 10-6;
Easter weekend and Suns,
10-3.30

**Whitby** Pannett Park
Museum & Art Gallery
Oct-Apr, Mon, Tue, Thur
& Fri 10.30-4, Wed & Sat
10.30-5.30; May-Sep,
Mon-Sat 9.30-5.30, Sun
2-5.30

**Whitby** Sutcliffe Gallery
Mon-Sat 9-5 (Wed 9-12.30,
Oct-Apr)

**YORK** see p. 27

## Natural Features

Yorkshire's geology gives
rise to many unusual and
impressive physical
features. Some of these
beauty spots can only be
reached on foot: details of
access are in the Gazetteer.

**\*Aysgarth** Aysgarth Falls
Triple waterfalls on River
Ure

**\*Bempton Cliffs**
400ft high chalk cliffs (with
RSPB reserve)

**Bolton Abbey** Strid
Narrow defile on River
Wharfe

**\*Brimham Rocks** (NT)
Fantastic rock formations

**Filey** Filey Brigg
Coastal promontory

**Flamborough Head**
Coastal promontory

**Goathland** Mallyan Spout
Waterfall on West Beck

**Great Ayton** Roseberry
Topping (NT)
Sandstone peak

**Harrogate** Plompton Rocks
Fantastic rock formations

**Hawes** Buttertubs Pass
Limestone phenomenon

*****Hawes** Hardrow Force
100ft waterfall in Fossdale
Gill

*****Hole of Horcum**
Declivity at head of
Levisham Beck

**Ilkley** Cow & Calf Rocks
Curious millstone grit
formations

**Ilkley** Ilkley Moor
Moorland overlooking
Wharfedale

*****Ingleton** Gaping Gill
Cavern (pothole)

*****Ingleton** (Clapham)
Ingleborough Cave
Cavern with stalactites &
stalagmites
Mar-Oct, daily 10.30-5.30;
Nov-Feb, Sat & Sun
10.30-4.30

*****Ingleton** White Scar Caves
Floodlit caves
Daily from 10 am

**Keld** Kisdon Force
Triple waterfall on River
Swale

**Kilnsey** Kilnsey Crag
Limestone outcrop in
Wharfedale

**Knaresborough** Dropping
Well
Easter-Oct, from 10 am

**Lofthouse** How Stean Gorge
Fossil limestone defile

*****Malham** Malham Cove
Limestone cliff close to
source of River Aire

**Malham** Malham Tarn (NT)
Glacial lake close to source
of River Aire

*****Malham** Gordale Scar
Gorge with overhanging
rocks & waterfall

*****Newton Dale**
Glacial overflow channel on
North Yorkshire Moors

**Otley** Chevin
900-ft moorland escarpment

**Ravenscar** Coastal
promontory

**Semerwater**
Glacially-formed lake

**Staithes** Boulby Cliffs
(Cleveland)
666ft coastal cliffs, highest
in England

*****Stump Cross Caverns**
Caves with stalactites &
stalagmites
See *Museums, Galleries &
Visitor Centres*

**Sutton Bank** Gormire
'Bottomless' lake

**Thornton Dale** Bridestones
(NT)
Fantastic rock formations
on North Yorkshire Moors
(See also *Nature Reserves*)

**Whitby** Falling Foss
Woodland waterfall on
Little Beck

**Whitby** Saltwick Nab (NT)
Coastal promontory

# Nature Reserves

Yorkshire's strongly defined
geological features provide
much scope for study of
characteristic animal and
plant life. Most of the nature
reserves listed below are
managed by the Yorkshire
Wildlife Trust (YWT),
others by the Nature
Conservancy Council
(NCC), National Trust
(NT), Royal Society for
Nature Conservation
(RSNC) and Royal Society
for the Protection of Birds
(RSPB).
Addresses for information:
*Yorkshire Wildlife Trust* 20
Castlegate, York YO1 1RP,
Tel (0904) 59570
*Nature Conservancy Council*
Matmer House, Hull Road,
York YO1 3JW, Tel (0904)
412420
*National Trust* (regional
office) Goddards, 27
Tadcaster Road, York YO2
2QG, Tel (0904) 702021
*Royal Society for the
Protection of Birds* E Floor,
Milburn House, Dean
Street, Newcastle-upon-
Tyne NE1 1LE, Tel (0632)
324148
*Royal Society for Nature
Conservation* The Green,
Nettleham, Lincoln LN2
2NR Tel (0522) 752326

In the selection of nature
reserves listed, most give
free or limited access, but
permits are required for
some at certain times.

*****Bempton Cliffs** *Bempton
Cliffs Bird Reserve* (RSPB)
Chalk cliffs, seabirds

*****Farndale**
Natural area with daffodils

**Goathland** *Fen Bog*
40-acre reserve (YWT)

*****Grassington** *Grass Wood
Nature Reserve* (YWT)
Great Scar limestone cliff,
pavement, scree. Woodlands

**Hackness** *Forge Valley
Nature Reserve* (NCC)
Woodland valley on site of
old iron workings

**Hayburn Wyke** *Hayburn
Wyke Nature Reserve* (NT &
NCC)
Coastal woods and waterfall

**Ingleton** *Southerscales Scar
Nature Reserve* (RSNC)
Limestone pavement;
flowers and ferns

**Settle** *Ling Gill Nature
Reserve* (NCC)
Cliff-like crags; woods

**Settle** *South House
Pavement Nature Reserve*
(YWT)
Limestone pavement;
characteristic plants

**Sledmere House** *Wharram
Quarry Nature Reserve*
(YWT)
Chalk quarry site; plants,
butterflies

**Sutton Bank** *Garbutt Woods
Nature Reserve* (YWT)
Sandstone cliff; lakeshore:
bracken, bog and marsh
plants, badger and deer

**Thornton Dale** *Bridestones
Nature Reserve* (YWT &
NT)
Moorland rock formations;
heather and upland pasture;
deer

**YORK** see p. 27

# Hotels & Historic Inns

†Non-residential inn
(THF) A Trusthouse Forte
Hotel

## Guisborough

†*The Anchor Inn*
Belmangate
Tel (0287) 32715

This well-known inn stands
in one of Guisborough's
oldest streets and is quite
unspoiled, with traditional
small bars and stone-flagged
floors. Other original
features include open coal
fires and original hand
pumps. At the end of the
garden is a quoits pitch,
where league championship
matches are held.

## Harrogate

†*Crown Hotel* (THF)
Crown Place, Harrogate
Tel (0423) 67755

In a quiet situation near the
town centre by the Valley
Gardens, this former
coaching inn (visited by
Lord Byron) developed as a
hotel during Harrogate's
heyday as a Victorian spa.

*Hotel Majestic* (THF)
Ripon Road, Harrogate
Tel (0423) 68972

This grand hotel, dating
back to 1900, was another
that served visitors to
Harrogate's famous spa. Set
in extensive gardens, the
hotel offers a wide range of
leisure facilities.

## Helmsley

*The Black Swan* (THF)
Market Place
Tel (0439) 70466

The old coaching inn dates
from the Georgian period,
but the oak ceilings and
fireplaces are from the 16th
c. The inn has long served as
a local centre. Moorland
farmers brought their wool
here; venison from the
Duncombe Estate is served
at the estate's traditional
Rent Dinners, and the inn is
a meeting place for
Sinnington Hunt.

## Ilkley

*Craiglands Hotel* (THF)
Cowpasture Road, Ilkley
Tel (0943) 607676

Standing high above the
town in 9 acres of gardens,
commanding a fine view of
Wharfedale, this ivy-clad
Victorian hotel has been
extended and modernised as
a resort hotel, with easy
access to the many local
attractions including Ilkley
Moor, Bolton Abbey,
Malham Cove and the
Brontë country.

## Keld

†*The Tan Hill Inn*
Tel (0748) 28246

A moorland road climbs
from Keld to Tan Hill
(1732ft); a few inches over
the Durham border, *The
Tan Hill Inn* is the highest
licensed house in England.
It is a typical moorland
cottage of stone, with a slate
roof and a protective porch,
built as a miners' rest house
when Tan Hill was a coal
producing area.

## Knaresborough

†*Mother Shipton Inn*
Low Bridge, Knaresborough
Tel (0423) 862157

A white-washed country
inn, parts dating from the
16th c., near Mother
Shipton's Cave. Oil
paintings on the walls show
the cave and surrounding
countryside; the Oak Room
has a heavy wooden table
which belonged to Guy
Fawkes when he lived at
Scotton Hall in 1592.

## Malton

*Talbot Hotel* (THF)
Yorkersgate
Tel (0653) 4031

Thought to have originated
as a 'hunting box' – a house
used by the local meet – the
*Talbot* was converted to an
inn in the 18th c. The
elegant stone building,
situated at the entrance to
the old market town, is now
a modern hotel in spacious
terraced grounds, which
maintains the style of a
period country house.

## Northallerton

*Golden Lion Hotel* (THF)
Market Place
Tel (0609) 2404

Dating from at least the
Tudor period, this
handsome inn was rebuilt in
its day as a prosperous
staging post. At its peak the
stables housed 60 horses and
supplied teams for coaches
travelling a 23m stretch
along the York-Scotland
highway. Of the same date is
the bar 'mess', a private
room then reserved for
barristers and magistrates
staying at the inn to prevent
the public from corrupting
or intimidating them.

## Pickering

*Saltersgate Inn*
Near Pickering
Tel (0751) 60236

Built in 1648, this venerable
inn was a staging post for
horses on the Whitby-York
run. It was also a smugglers'
hideout for illicit salt trading
to evade the salt tax, and it is
from this practice that the
inn got its name. Two salt
cupboards can be seen in the
bar, which was formerly the
kitchen; a peat fire here is
said to have been burning
unextinguished since 1801.
Beneath the fireplace, it is
claimed, lies the body of a
too-honest landlord who
betrayed the smugglers and
was killed in revenge. His
small daughter was turned
out on to the moors on a
winter's night, and the
soughing of the moorland
wind can at times sound like
a child weeping. Her mother
is the inn's resident
(benevolent) ghost.

## Thirsk

*The Golden Fleece* (THF)
Market Place
Tel (0845) 23108

Early in the 19th c. the inn
took over the coaching trade
of *The Three Tuns* whose
landlady was a relative of
George Blyth, then landlord
of *The Golden Fleece*. He
extended the inn, and built
up the stables which later
accommodated 60 horses.

## Famous Connections

Many famous – or simply unusual – personalities have been connected with this region of Yorkshire. Details of their association will be found in the Gazetteer entries.

**Baltimore, 2nd Lord** Bolton-on-Swale (Kiplin Hall)

**Brontë, Anne** Scarborough

**Brontë family** Skipton (Haworth)

**Buckingham, George Villiers, 2nd Duke of** Bilsdale, Kirkbymoorside

**Cayley, Sir George** Scarborough (Brompton)

**Charles I** York

**Chippendale, Thomas** Otley

**Clifford, Lady Anne** Barden Tower, Skipton

**Clitherow, Margaret** (St Margaret of York) York

**Constantine the Great** York

**Cook, Captain James** Great Ayton (Marton), Staithes, Whitby

**Coverdale, Miles** East Witton (Caldbergh)

**Cradock, Rear Admiral Sir Christopher** Richmond

**Cromwell, Oliver** Coxwold, Marston Moor, Ripley

**Edward II** Byland Abbey

**Edward IV** Middleham

**Edwin of Northumbria** York

**Fairfax, Thomas, Lord** Ilkley (Denton Hall), Marston Moor, York

**Fawkes, Guy** Otley (Farnley Hall), York

**Greathead, Henry** Richmond

**Harewood, Earl of** Harewood House

**Herriot, James** Pickering, Reeth, Thirsk, York

**Hudson, George** York

**Hume, Basil, Cardinal Archbishop of Westminster** Ampleforth

**I'anson, Frances** Richmond

**Kearton, Cherry & Richard** Thwaite (Muker)

**Kent, Duchess of** Hovingham

**Kingsley, Charles** Arncliffe, Kirkby Malham, Malham

**Knight, Dame Laura** Staithes

**Lambert, John ('Honest John')** Kirkby Malham

**Lawrence of Arabia** (Aircraftsman Shaw) Bridlington

**Lord, Thomas** Thirsk

**Mary, Queen of Scots** Bolton Castle, Leyburn, Ripon

**Neville, Richard, Earl of Warwick** (the 'Kingmaker') Middleham

**Parr, Catherine** Danby, Nun Monkton, Snape

**Paulinus, Bishop of York** Catterick Bridge, York

**Richard II** Knaresborough, Pickering

**Richard III** Middleham, Sheriff Hutton

**Rupert of the Rhine, Prince** Marston Moor, York

**St Hilda** Whitby

**St Wilfrid** Ripon

**Scoresby, Captain William** (father and son) Whitby

**Scott, Sir Walter** West Tanfield

**Shipton, Mother** Knaresborough

**Sitwell family** Scarborough

**Sterne, Lawrence** Coxwold

**Stoker, Bram** Whitby

**Sutcliffe, Frank Meadows** Whitby

**Turner, J.M.W** Otley (Farnley Hall)

**Turpin, Dick** York

**Walmsley, Leo** Robin Hood's Bay

**Wordsworth, William & Mary** Scarborough (Brompton)

**Wyclif, John** Richmond (Hipswell)

**Thackeray, William Makepeace** Hampsthwaite

## Festivals and Events

Many colourful events, from village fairs and local agricultural shows to international arts festivals, take place throughout the region. For events in **York**, see p. 26. Some of the most popular events elsewhere are:

**Easter** *Harrogate* International Youth Music Festival, Model Railway Exhibition

**April** *Harrogate* Flower Show (2nd week)

**May** *Harrogate* Arts & Crafts Market; *Ilkley* Wharfedale Music Festival (2nd/3rd week); *Whitby* Planting of the Penny Hedge

**June** *Harrogate* Cricket Festival, Hallé Orchestra Festival (3rd week), International Festival of Cycling; *Ilkley* Literature Festival (biennial); *Knaresborough* Bed Race; *Masham* Steam Engine & Fair Organ Rally; *Scarborough* International Festival; *Whitby* Music, Drama & Arts Festival

**July** *Bridlington* Dance Festival; *Filey* Edwardian Festival (1st week); *Harrogate* Great Yorkshire Show (2nd week); *Ilkley* Ballet Seminar (Jul/Aug); *Pickering* Carnival (1st or 2nd week), Traction Engine Rally (last week); *Ripon* St Wilfrid's Feast (last week)

**August** *Bridlington* RYYC Regatta; *Burnsall* Feast Day; *Egton Bridge* Old Gooseberry Show (1st Tue); *Harrogate* International Festival of Music & Arts (1st & 2nd weeks); *Helmsley* Festival (1st week); *Ilkley* Ballet Seminar, Open Lawn Tennis Tournament (early); *Ripon* Feast of St Wilfrid (1st week); *West Witton* Burning Bartle (1st Sat after Aug 24); *Whitby* Regatta (3rd week), Folk Festival (week before Summer Bank Hol)

**September** *Bridlington* Angling Festival; *Harrogate* Flower Show (2nd week), Northern Antique Dealers' Fair (3rd/4th week); *Scarborough* Carnival (2nd & 3rd week), Cricket Festival, International Motor Cycle Races

## Sport & Recreation

**Boating** Knaresborough on the Nidd, Ilkley and Otley on the Wharfe, York on the Ouse and Ruswarp and Sleights on the Esk provide excellent opportunities for hiring rowing boats and canoes. Skipton on the Leeds & Liverpool Canal is a good centre for barge and motor boat cruising in both directions, but negotiating locks is a necessary feature, and it is advisable to book well ahead; daily motor boat cruises lasting 1hr are also available.

At Whitby, Scarborough and Bridlington, motor boat trips are organised by local fishermen, and cruise vessels operate for longer distances along the coast from Scarborough and Bridlington. Yachting is popular at all three resorts, at Thruscross Reservoir near Pateley Bridge, and on flooded gravel pits near Otley.

**Fishing** Coarse and trout fishing are available on the rivers and many of the reservoirs, and salmon fishing on the Esk; full information can be obtained from the numerous angling clubs throughout the region, and from the Yorkshire Water Authority, West Riding House, 67 Albion Street, Leeds LS1 5AA, Tel (0532) 448201. Sea fishing is popular from the piers and rocks along the coast, and boats can be chartered from fishermen.

**Fell Walking, Rock Climbing & Caving** Fell walking is popular in the upper reaches of the Dales with their high botanical and geological interest; rock climbing, caving and pot-holing are also popular in the limestone districts of the Dales. Main centres are at Kettlewell and Grassington in Wharfedale, Pateley Bridge in Nidderdale, Malham in Malhamdale, Settle in Ribblesdale and Ingleton (with Clapham) further W.

**Gliding** The Yorkshire Gliding Club's Headquarters are at Sutton Bank, and all grades are taught. Hang gliding is practised at Arncliffe, Ilkley and the Hole of Horcum, and powered hang gliding at the disused Wombleton Airfield near Helmsley. Further details from local Tourist Information Centres, or the Yorkshire & Humberside Tourist Board (see p. 25).

**Golf** Many golf clubs throughout the region offer a welcome to non-members; Fulford (near York), Pannal (near Harrogate) and Ganton (near Scarborough) have achieved Championship status. Details are available from Tourist Information Centres, or from the Yorkshire & Humberside Tourist Board (see p. 25).

**Riding** Hacking and pony trekking are available for experienced and novice riders, particularly along the coast and in the vicinity of the North York Moors. Opportunities are fewer in the Dales. Regular flat race meetings are held at Catterick Bridge, Ripon, Thirsk, Wetherby (near Harrogate) and York. Details can be obtained from Tourist Information Centres, or the Yorkshire & Humberside Tourist Board (see p. 25).

**Forests** Forestry Commission properties have picnic areas, waymarked trails, forest walks and other recreational opportunities; some of the best known are described in the Gazetteer. Below are listed names of principal forest areas as designated by the Forestry Commission (see also *North Yorkshire Forests*).

Further details are available from the Forestry Commission Office at 42/43 Eastgate, Pickering YO18 7DU, Tel (0751) 72771/73810, from the Tourist Information Centre at Pickering, or from the Visitor Centre near Thornton Dale (see below).

**Cleveland Hills** *Cleveland Forest*
Viewpoints and picnic areas

**Helmsley** *Hambleton Forest*
Viewpoint, picnic areas, walks

**Pickering** *Cropton Forest*
Walks, pony trekking; Information, North York Moors Railway

**Scarborough** *Wykeham Forest*
Picnic areas, walks

**Thornton Dale** *Dalby Forest*
Forest drive, lake, nature reserve, Visitor & Information Centre (see *Museums, Galleries & Visitor Centres*)

## Walks

Both National Parks abound in walks which offer good circular routes through a wide variety of scenery.

On the fells and moors, where weather conditions are extremely changeable, basic fell walking safety rules should always be followed. Care should be taken, also, to follow the Country Code and to remember that routes of designated walks like the Cleveland or the Pennine Ways follow ancient rights of way across privately-owned land.

**Long-Distance Walks** The *Pennine Way* and the *Dalesway* in the Dales, the *Cleveland Way* and the *Lyke Wake Walk* in the North York Moors are the major walks. which cover sections of the National Parks. Other walks in the region are the *Ebor Way* and the *Wolds Way*. HMSO has published some useful booklets on three of the major walks with OS maps reproduced full-size and details of the routes: *The Cleveland Way* by Alan Falconer, *The Pennine Way* by Tom Stephenson and *The Wolds Way* by Roger Ratcliffe. *The Dalesman* has two useful publications entitled *The Cleveland Way* and *The Lyke Wake Walk*. Details can also be obtained from National Park Information Centres (see p. 25).

The following walks comprise three in the Dales Park – one each in Airedale, Wharfedale and Swaledale; and three in the Moors Park – two inland and one coastal: they are typical of the numerous routes available. They should be followed with the help of a 1:50 000 or a 1:25 000 scale map.

**Walk 1** *Malham to Malham Cove in Airedale*
From the car park in the village turn left past the Information Centre, cross the bridge, turn left at *The Lister's Arms* and walk past the YHA hostel. Then up the lane; take the left of two gates and continue straight on until the Cove is reached. Pass below it and then take the steps 300ft to the top; climb over the stone wall and descend to Malham Beck. Here join a path, part of the Pennine Way, which returns to Malham/3m

**Walk 2** *To Appletreewick in Wharfedale*
Park 2m E of Hebden on B6265 at a
Yorkshire Water Authority signpost,
'Grimwith Reservoir'. Proceed
downhill to Dibbles End Bridge, then
uphill to a farm, 'Turf Gate House' (on
the left). Pass through a yard and by a
concrete shed with a wall on the right;
continue past a barn on the right and
follow a wall on the left. Then over a
stile and across a field to another stile,
before dropping down to a stream by
bearing right through a gap in a wall.
Continue over two more stiles with a
wall on the left before crossing the
water and climbing Langerton Hill
with a wall on the right.

Join the road at Raikes House Farm;
go downhill and left into Hartlington,
then past Woodhouse Farm to join a
river path to Appletreewick. Follow the
track W of *The Craven Arms* past the
stocks, and at the end bear right at a
field corner and proceed diagonally
across the field. Go through two gates
and continue for ½m with a wall on the
left; cross a bridge and go past a sheep
fold. Proceed across a field towards a
house and without losing height bear
right towards a stile above a wood after
crossing a stream. Then continue to a
gateway in a wall, cross a stile to B6265
and turn right to the car park/5m

**Walk 3** *Around Richmond in Swaledale*
From the market place go downhill
beside Richmond Castle; cross the
bridge upstream and go through an
opening on the right onto the river
bank. Follow the track into Hadswell
Woods and after climbing steps take
the lower right fork where the path
divides; carry straight on to the wood
bottom and cross the stile ahead.
Continue across pastureland between
the river and Round Howe, and at a
picnic area cross a footbridge and turn
left along A6108. Then turn right onto
a farm track, passing in front of the
house to a gate into a wood.

Pass through the wood and leave by a
gate, following the line of the wood
beside the stream to join the river
beyond a dilapidated wall. Continue
over a stile to the edge of a field. Turn
right, cross another stile and continue
along the field side to a gate to join the
waymarked route through gates, round

and to the left of a farm, and uphill to a
waymarked stile on the right. Three
more stiles lead to East Applegarth
Farm, but before reaching the house go
through a gate and turn left round the
house to join a path and pass through a
gate and stile into Whitcliffe Wood.
Then join the lane and cross a stile into
parkland, keeping parallel with the
road into town. Cross the A6108 back
to the market place/7m

**Walk 4** *Rievaulx and Old Byland in*
*Ryedale*
Park ¼m S of the village by the Rye and
continue to the 'T' junction. Turn right
over the bridge and continue 1m
towards Scawton to a Cleveland Way
signpost. Turn right through a gate and
follow a forest road past three ponds to
a gate into Rievaulx Forest. The road
bears right for 1½m to a tarmac road,
then right into Old Byland. Beyond the
village turn left towards Hawnby and
right at the next junction, then along an
'Unsuitable' signposted road downhill
to a belt of pines. Turn right through a
gate to Caydale Mill, then go along a
bridleway parallel to the beck past
another bridleway sign. Pass through a
gate and woodland towards Tylas
Farm.

Pass along the tarmac road away
from the farm to the stream at the
bottom of the hill, go through a gate
and across a field to the river. Then go
downstream to a stile and on to a
poorly-surfaced lane. Turn left here
over Bow Bridge and cross a stile near
some large trees on the right to reach
the river, then cross two more stiles and
go straight on to the Abbey. Pass
through two gates to the right of a stone
building and follow the road through
the village until the starting point is
reached/8½m

**Walk 5** *Troutsdale*
Start from the car park ¼m N of
Cockmoor Hall on the road running N
from Snainton on A170. Follow the
rough road through a gate and
alongside part of Wykeham Forest to
the road, and continue 1m to the
Hackness road. Turn left to Troutsdale
Low Hall and then right close to a
timber garage, and follow an
'Unsuitable' road to Freeze Gill Farm.
Behind this a track rises steeply before

passing through woodland to Backleys Farm. After passing to the right of a house, bear left behind buildings to a gate marked 'Right of Way' and proceed to a stile on a forest road.

Follow the road to the left as far as a clearing on the left; turn left again onto another road down into a dale, and join a tarmac road to continue uphill to the car park/9m

**Walk 6** *Ravenscar and Hayburn Wyke*
Start at the car park near the *Raven Hall Hotel* at Ravenscar. After bearing right at the hotel entrance, turn left at the Cleveland Way signpost. At the cliff edge, turn right for a 3½m walk to Hayburn Wyke where the path crosses a bridge near the shoreline. Go straight on and climb through a wood, passing right of a Nature Reserve sign until the incline levels out, where a right turn should be made downhill to a bridge over Hayburn Beck. The path continues on the beckside, then climbs to the top of a wood to meet a farm track. Turn left here to the end of the track and right along a surfaced road to its end, where a track to Plane Tree Farm should be followed. Passing to the right of the buildings the path continues beyond White Hall Farm through a gate to the entrance to Prospect House Farm; here a left turn is made for Ravenscar Church then right along the road to the car park/8½m

## Motoring Tours

These six motoring tours take in the best features of the region. Each is circular, and can be started at any point. Names in brackets indicate places of interest on or near the route. OS 1″ to the mile maps to the two National Parks are recommended; allow the best part of a day for each tour.

**Tour 1** *Richmond, Reeth, Redmire, Aysgarth, Leyburn, Masham, Bedale*
Richmond – W along A6108 onto B6270 for Grinton (Maiden Castle W) – left and then right along minor road over Grinton Moor, through Castle Bolton (castle) to Carperby (W) – left to A684 and right to Aysgarth (Aysgarth Falls) – return along A684 through

Wensley to Leyburn – right on A6108 to Masham and over Ure onto B6267 at Low Burton – then left onto B6268 for Bedale – left onto A684 to Leyburn and right along A6108 to Richmond/65m

**Tour 2** *Ripon to Pateley Bridge and through Wharfedale to Harrogate and Knaresborough*
Ripon – W along B6265 (Brimham Rocks) to Pateley Bridge and continue (past Stump Cross Caverns on Greenhow Hill) to Grassington – left over bridge and right to take B6160 (Burnsall, Appletreewick diversion, Barden Tower) to Bolton Abbey – then left to Bolton Bridge to join A59 for Harrogate – follow A59 out of town and to Knaresborough – left onto B6165 to join A61 at Ripley – right to Ripon/68m

**Tour 3** *York to Knaresborough and minor roads for Fountains Abbey, Wharfedale, Malham and Harrogate*
York – on A59 to Knaresborough (pass Nun Monkton to right) – right onto B6165 and right again at roundabout on A61 (Ripley Castle) – ahead at next roundabout onto B6165, then right and right again on minor roads for Markington, then left and right to Fountains Abbey – back across river and right fork, then right again for Sawley; right to join B6265 near Risplith – left to Crossgates and left again on minor road past Brimham Rocks to crossroads – right to join B6165 at Wilsill and on to Pateley Bridge – left onto B6265 to Grassington (via Greenhow Hill and Stump Cross Caverns) – right onto minor road on E side of Wharfe to Conistone (past Grass Wood Nature Reserve), then left and across bridge and right onto B6160 through Kilnsey (Kilnsey Crag on left) and left to Arncliffe in Littondale (wild limestone scenery up-dale) – left along moorland roads past Malham Tarn into Malham – then ahead to Airton – left to B6265 and on to Linton – right onto B6160 to join A59 at Bolton Bridge – ahead to Harrogate and A61, which cross at A661 for Wetherby – over Wharfe – left at roundabout onto A1 and shortly right onto minor roads through Wighill, Askham Richard and Askham Bryan to York/132m

**Tour 4** *Stokesley and Bilsdale, Cleveland Hills and Eskdale: from Captain Cook country in Staithes to Great Ayton*
Stokesley – A172 towards Thirsk – turn 2nd left through Carlton and up into Cleveland Hills to B1257 – left and take 3rd right along moorland road for Ingleby Greenhow, through Battersby and right for Kildale – proceed to Commondale, turn right to Castleton and through Danby, then left to A171 – right past Scaling Dam and 2nd left onto B1266 – left through Ellerby and across A174 to Runswick Bay – rejoin A174 at Hinderwell and take 2nd right to Staithes (Captain Cook) – rejoin A174 and proceed right to Brotton (Boulby Cliff on right) and left onto A173 for Guisborough (Guisborough Priory), Great Ayton (Captain Cook) and Stokesley/57m

**Tour 5** *Scarborough to Esk Dale: across moors to Rosedale and Farndale; through Hutton-le-Hole to Thornton Dale and Dalby Forest Drive*
Scarborough – A171 through Scalby to Burniston – for 9m through Cloughton to B1416 – left to five-way intersection – continue along main road, then left and right to Ugglebarnby and Sleights – left onto A169 and right across Black Brow (view) to Grosmont and Egton – left to Egton Bridge across Esk and straight on across Egton High Moor – straight on to Rosedale Abbey – right at cross-roads, right again then left to 'T' junction at dale head (view: 'Fat Betty' wayside cross marked as White Cross on OS map, & Ralph Cross) – left along Blakey Ridge and right to Church Houses in Farndale – left to rejoin Blakey Ridge at 'T' junction – right into Hutton-le-Hole (Ryedale Folk Museum) and left to Lastingham – left at first 'T' junction and right at second one to Cropton (Cawthorn Roman Camps to E) and on through Wrelton to A170 – left to Pickering and Thornton Dale – left at cross-roads onto A169 – second turning right for Dalby Forest Drive (toll road) through Low Dalby (Dalby Forest Visitor Centre) and on to Langdale End – then to third 'T' junction, at which turn left (Forge Valley to right) through Hackness and Suffield – right to Scalby on A171 and right to Scarborough/79m

**Tour 6** *Whitby through Esk Dale to Westerdale; Farndale and around Bransdale to Helmsley; via Kirk Dale to Kirkbymoorside and Pickering, and N through Goathland*
Whitby – A174 to Sandsend and Lythe – left for Ugthorpe and A171 – left and right to Lealholm in Esk Dale – follow dale road W to Danby (go past Danby Lodge National Park Centre) and on to Castleton and Westerdale – left along valley to 'T' junction (Ralph Cross, view) – right and right again along Blakey Ridge to right turn (view) for Church Houses in Farndale; cross river and turn left to Low Mill, bear right for Gillamoor (view) – right up Bransdale to Cockayne at dale head – skirt head and turn S along Lund Ridge and through Riccall Dale to Helmsley – left on A170 through twin villages of Beadlam and Nawton – leave main road as it bears sharply right and continue straight to Kirk Dale and St Gregory's Minster, then on to rejoin A170, at which left for Kirkbymoorside and Pickering – left at roundabout onto A169 for Hole of Horcum – on to Eller Beck Bridge (Fen Bog Nature Reserve, Fylingdales Early Warning Station Lilla Howe) where fork left for Goathland (waterfalls) – rejoin A169 – turn left down Blue Bank to Sleights – across bridge and right on B1410 to Ruswarp – left at 'T' junction up Ruswarp Bank to roundabout – either straight on, or turn right into Whitby/80m

**Further Information** Information on the National Parks and on leisure activities in the region is available in booklets, leaflets and information sheets put out by the Yorkshire & Humberside Tourist Board, 312 Tadcaster Road, York YO2 2HF, Tel (0904) 707961.
Maps and publications can also be obtained from main information offices of the National Park authorities: the North York Moors National Park at The Old Vicarage, Bondgate, Helmsley, Tel (0439) 70657; and the Yorkshire Dales National Park at Colvend, Hebden Road, Grassington, Tel (0756) 752748. Other National Park Information Centres are shown in the Gazetteer.

# The City of York

Population 104,750

**Tourist Information** De Grey Rooms, Exhibition Square Tel York (0904) 21756/7. Apr-Oct, Mon-Sat 9-8, Sun 2-5; Nov-Mar, Mon-Sat 9.5. Also 'What's On in York' Tel (0904) 28556, May-Sep

**Post Office** Lendal

**Shopping** Blake Street; Church Street; Colliergate; Coney Street; Coppergate; Davygate; Goodramgate; High & Low Petergate; King's Square; Market Street; New Street; Parliament Street; Shambles; Spurriergate; Stonegate. (Early closing Wed)

**Market Day** Mon-Sat

**Theatre** Theatre Royal, St Leonard's Place. Tel (0904) 23568

**Events** York Festival & Mystery Plays (Jun, every 4th year: next 1988); Early Music Festival (Jul); Antique Fair (Oct)

**Tours** *Walking* 2hr conducted tours from Exhibition Square, Good Fri-Oct, daily at 10.15 & 2.15, also Jun-Aug 7.15. *Bus* Jorvik Tour: starting Castle Museum; hourly tours with pick-up points throughout city centre. Also courier-conducted coach tours, Apr-Oct, starting from Royal York Hotel (Tel 24161). *River* From Hills Boatyard, Lendal Bridge (Tel 23752) Apr-Sep, to Bishopthorpe Palace; City cruises also offered in season by Ouse Cruises (Tel 32530) and White Rose Line (Tel 28324)

**Places of Interest**
*Descriptions of these places are given in the Walk, which follows. See Index for page references*

*Churches*

**\*York Minster**
Open from 7am daily; varied closing times. Chapter House and other special features open from 10am daily, 1pm Sun; varied closing times. No sightseeing during services

**\*All Saints** North Street

**All Saints** Pavement

**\*Holy Trinity** Goodramgate

**St Mary** Castlegate (The York Story) *See Museums, Galleries & Exhibition Centres*

**St Michael-le-Belfrey** Minster Yard

**St Olave** Marygate

*Historic Buildings*

**Assembly Rooms** Blake Street Mon-Fri 10-4 (except when in use)

**Clifford's Tower** Tower Street mid Mar-mid Oct, Mon-Sat 9.30-6.30 (also Apr-Sep, Sun); mid Oct-mid Mar, Mon-Sat 9.30-4, Sun 2-4. Closed 1-2

**Fairfax House** Castlegate Apr-Sep, Tue-Sat 11-5, Sun 1.30-5; Nov-Mar, closed at dusk

**Guildhall** St Helen's Square May-Oct, Mon-Thur 9-5, Fri 9-4.30, Sat 10-5; Oct-Apr closed Sat

**King's Manor** Exhibition Square Courtyard open daily. Public Rooms on application to Porter's Lodge

**Mansion House** St Helen's Square Mon-Fri, by arrangement

**Merchant Adventurers' Hall** Fossgate Apr-Oct, daily 9.30-1, most afternoons until 4; Nov-Mar, Mon-Sat 9.30-1

**Merchant Taylors' Hall** Aldwark May-Sep, Mon-Sat 10-4

**St Anthony's Hall** Peasholme Green Mon-Sat 9.30-1 & 2-5 (by appointment only)

**St Mary's Abbey** Museum Gardens

**St William's College** College Street
Mon-Sat 10-6 (5 in winter), Sun
12.30-6 (5 in winter)

**Treasurer's House** (NT) Minster Yard
Apr-Oct, 10.30-6

*Museums, Galleries & Exhibition Centres*

**Castle Museum**
Apr-Sep, Mon-Sat 9.30-6.30, Sun
10-6.30. Oct-Mar, Mon-Sat 9.30-5,
Sun 10-5 (last admission one hour
before closure)

**City Art Gallery** Exhibition Square
Mon-Sat 10-5, Sun 2.30-5

**Friargate Wax Museum** Lower
Friargate
Apr-Sep, daily 10-7; Oct-Mar, daily
10-5.30

**Jorvik Viking Centre** Coppergate
Apr-Oct, daily 9-7; Nov-Mar, daily
9-5.30

**Rail Riders World** York Station
Daily 10-6

**National Railway Museum** Leeman
Road
Mon-Sat 10-6, Sun 2.30-6

**Regimental Museum** (West Yorkshire
Regiment) Imphal Barracks, Fulford
Road
Mon-Fri 9.30-12.30 & 2-4

**Yorkshire Museum** Museum Gardens
Mon-Sat 10-5, Sun 1-5

**Yorkshire Museum of Farming**
Murton (3m E of city)
Apr-Oct, daily 10.30-6

**York Story** St Mary's Church,
Castlegate
Mon-Sat 10-5, Sun 1-5

*Parks & Gardens*

**Museum Gardens**
Mon-Fri 7.30-dusk, Sat 8-dusk, Sun
10-dusk

**Moorlands Nature Reserve**
Off A19 6m NW of York, 2m NE of
Skelton
This Yorkshire Wildlife Trust reserve
has native woodland and exotica, with
colourful displays in season.

*Hotels & Historic Inns*

†Non-residential inn
(THF) A Trusthouse Forte Hotel

*Black Swan Inn*
Peasholme Green
Tel (0904) 25236
This timber-framed building, with
carved barge boards and overhanging
upper storeys, is one of the sights of old
York. Equally attractive is the interior,
which includes a room with medieval
painted panels and a Delft tile fireplace.
In the 16th c. the inn was the home of
the Bowes family: William, father and
son, both being Lord Mayors of the
city.

*Judges' Lodging*
9 Lendal
Tel (0904) 23587/38733
The house was built in 1720 by William
Kent for a successful doctor: the stone
head over the central doorway
represents Aesculapius, God of
Healing. From 1806-1976 the house
was the official residence of the Judges
of Assize during their visits to York. It
has since been attractively converted
into a residential hotel with a restaurant
and bar.

†*Roman Bath*
St Sampson's Square
Tel (0904) 20455
This appropriately-named inn stands
on the site of a Roman bath and
hypocaust, which can be seen by
looking down on the foundations
through an observation chamber in the
lounge bar. Some of the relics from the
site are on display.

†*Ye Olde Starre Inne*
40 Stonegate
Tel (0904) 23063
The city's oldest-established inn dates
from at least 1644, and the agreement
for the beam sign across Stonegate from
1733. The building is, however, more
recent, and has as its most attractive
feature the fine Victorian bar.

*Post House Hotel* (THF)
Tadcaster Road
Tel (0904) 707921
Executive Rooms are a feature of this
well-appointed hotel SW of the city.

*Clifford's Tower*

In 71AD, during their campaign against the Brigantian tribe, which dominated much of northern Britain, the Romans set up camp at the confluence of two rivers, the Ouse and the Foss. The camp became a fortress and subsequently one of the most important cities of the Roman Empire (Eboracum). It was Hadrian's base during his northern campaigns, and two other emperors died in the city: Septimius Severus (211) and Constantius Chlorus (306). The latter's death set the scene for an historic event: Constantius' son Constantine, who was with him at the time, was proclaimed Roman Emperor in the city. He later became Constantine the Great, the first Christian emperor and founder of Constantinople.

After the Romans' departure the city was much fought over and eventually became a Saxon settlement. This period saw another significant event in the history of the city when Bishop Paulinus, whose mission was to establish the Roman church in northern Britain, baptised King Edwin of Northumbria in a little timber church built for the purpose. This was in 627: in 633 Paulinus became first Archbishop of York and the church the first Minster.

In the 7th c. St Peter's School, from which the modern school of that name is descended, was founded by Paulinus. The great educationalist and theologian Alcuin was headmaster in the 8th c. A dramatic change befell the city when it was occupied by the Danes (867). Record of Viking York (Jorvik) is in the many street names ending in 'gate', derived from a Scandinavian word meaning 'street'.

In 944 Edmund drove out the Danes and re-established Anglo-Saxon rule. After Tostig and Harald Hardrada had been defeated by King Harold at Stamford Bridge (1066), 6m E of the city, and Harold himself defeated a few day later at Hastings by William the Conqueror, the Normans took possession of the city, overcoming all opposition by their devastation of the area and their construction of two motte and bailey castles (at Baile Hill and on the site of

*Micklegate Bar*

Clifford's Tower). By the 13th c. the city's present walls and gates, known as 'bars', were under construction and the place began to prosper as a trading centre and port. Guilds were established, many of them still being in existence today. York's tradition as one of England's main religious centres was maintained by the foundation of an abbey and priory and many churches. Its status as the northern capital of England was recognised by the monarchy by the granting of the title 'Duke of York' to the sovereign's second son. (The first recipient of the title was Edmund Langley, 1341-1402, son of Edward III.)

Decline set in with Henry VIII's Dissolution of the Monasteries, which caused severe depredation and loss to the city's many religious houses. The political importance of the city was however maintained, by the establishment here of the King's Council of the North, sitting at the King's Manor (the old abbot's house of St Mary's Abbey). The Roman Catholic cause was sub-sequently supported, in very different ways, by two natives of York: Guy Fawkes and Margaret Clitherow. Guy Fawkes, executed for his part in the Gunpowder Plot (1605), was born in a house in Petergate, on, or near to, the site of Young's Hotel, and was educated at St Peter's School. He was baptised in the Church of St Michael-le-Belfrey beside the Minster. Margaret Clitherow, a butcher's wife, was condemned to death in 1586 for allegedly harbouring Jesuit priests in her house in the Shambles; she was canonized as St Margaret of York in 1970.

During the Civil War the Parliamentarians besieged the city which was strongly pro-Royalist, having been the court of Charles I for three years (1639-42) after the king's flight from London. The siege was lifted by Prince Rupert of the Rhine but, after pursuing the retreating Commonwealth troops to Marston Moor, his forces were routed and put to flight. Reprisals by the Parliamentarians against the city were fortunately held in check by one of their generals, Sir Thomas Fairfax. Fairfax was a local man, and it is to him that the salvation of the precious stained glass and fabric of York's churches is due.

In the 18th c. the city saw a revival when it became a centre of Georgian fashion: the racecourse, Assembly Rooms and many elegant houses were built at this time. The Industrial Revolution barely touched York, but it became a great railway centre due to the enterprise of George Hudson, who became Lord Mayor and was one of the earliest railway investors of the 1830s-40s. Probably the best known of the city's industrial companies are the old-established confectionery firms of Rowntree and Terry. In 1963 the University was inaugurated from the nucleus of Heslington Hall on the E outskirts of the city.

York's vivid history is matched by the grandeur of its buildings, which can be particularly appreciated from the city walls and at night from Lendal Bridge, when the principal monuments are floodlit.

*Stonegate*

* **Walking tour** York's street pattern is based on the original Roman plan, with two main streets, the Via Praetoria and Via Principia meeting at the centre of the rectangle of the old Roman fortress. These two streets exist today as Stonegate and Petergate: at their junction on the site of the Roman Principia (the legionary headquarters) is the city's most splendid monument, the starting point of the tour.

**York Minster** (Cathedral Church of St Peter) Seat of the Archbishop of York, and cathedral church of the diocese of York, the Minster is the city's most imposing structure. It is the largest Gothic church in England: 524ft long, 249ft wide across the transepts and 90ft high. The twin W towers are 184ft and the central (lantern) tower 234ft high. The Minster took 250 years to build, from 1220-1472. It stands on the site of an earlier Norman structure *c.* 1080, which itself replaced a successor to the original timber church in which King Edwin of Northumbria was baptised.

*\*Note*: This tour is not feasible if all the museums, churches and houses are to be properly visited. It is suggested that the tour is split over two days, the first tour ending at and including the Jorvik Viking Centre, the second tour starting at Castlegate and including the Castle Museum.

The long period of its building is demonstrated by the different styles of the Minster's Gothic architecture. The oldest part of the Gothic rebuilding (Archbishop de Grey) is the S transept (damaged by fire in July 1984) which was completed in 1240: both this and the N transept, completed in 1260, are in the Early English style. The Chapter House, in the Decorated style, was completed in 1300 and the nave, also Decorated, in 1338. The Perpendicular choir was completed in 1450 and the twin W towers by 1472. The 13th-c. central tower, which had collapsed in 1407, was rebuilt in 1480.

In the 1960s serious subsidence was discovered in the Minster's foundations and it was feared that the tower would collapse again. A massive restoration project was undertaken, involving the laying of new foundations of reinforced concrete. At a cost of £2 million, raised purely from donations, the building was saved. A recent setback was the fire which gutted the S transept: fortunately the Rose Window survived and restoration work is now in progress.

Earlier fires, in 1829 and 1840, caused severe damage to the choir and nave respectively: the timber vaults of both are replacements of those destroyed at the time.

*Tour* Of the Minster's many treasures, the greatest is its stained glass, which together with that of York's other parish churches forms England's greatest collection of medieval stained and painted glass. The most impressive of its 128 windows are described in the sequence of a tour commencing at the W entrance

At the centre of the *nave* a good view is obtained of the W window, with its curvilinear Decorated tracery in the shape of a heart (the 'Heart of Yorkshire'). In the *N aisle* (2nd bay) the window contains a panel of stained glass (*c.* 1150) from the Norman building: in the 5th bay a window showing St Peter attended by pilgrims (*c.* 1312) has fascinating details in the lower border, including a monkey's funeral. In the S *aisle* (3rd bay) is a fine Jesse window.

Proceeding to the crossing, two of the Minster's finest windows can be admired. The splendid 16th-c. *Rose Window* in the S transept, consisting of no less than 17,000 pieces of glass, commemorates the marriage of Henry VII and Elizabeth of York in 1486, a union which signified the end of the Wars of the Roses. The *Five Sisters Window* in the N transept is named after its five lofty lancets, each over 50ft high and glazed with 13th-c. grisaille glass in geometric patterns. This window was releaded in 1925 as a memorial to the service women who gave their lives in World War I. Another feature which can be admired at the crossing is the elaborate 15th-c. stone *choir screen* with carved figures of English kings from William I to Henry VI. The vault of the *lantern tower*, above, has a central boss 4ft 9in wide showing St Peter with the Church and Keys of Heaven, and St Paul with sword and gospels.

In the *N transept* is a *clock* with two carved wooden figures, 400 years old, which strike the hours and quarters. Nearby is an *astronomical clock*, a memorial to 18,000 airmen based in the NE who perished in World War II. Also in the transept, on the W side, is *St John's Chapel*, dedicated to the King's Own Yorkshire Light Infantry.

Off the transept, through a majestic vestibule, is the entrance to the **Chapter House**, a remarkable octagonal building with a conical roof which relies on external buttresses to offset the thrust of the roof on the walls. This obviates the need for a central pillar, a common feature of this type of building.

The *choir*, entered from the N choir aisle, is a restoration following the 1829 fire: the choir stalls are 19th-c. replicas of the 15th-c. originals. Note the Archbishop's throne or *cathedra* (S side) from which the Minster derives its cathedral status. The *N* and *S choir aisles* have tombs and monuments to various archbishops and one prince: the 10-year-old William, second son of Edward III and Philippa of Hainault who were married in the Minster in 1328.

The E end of the Minster is dominated by the magnificent *Great E window* (78ft x 31ft). The work of John Thornton of Coventry (1405) it is the largest area of medieval stained glass in a single window in the world. The theme is 'The Beginning and The End', the upper panels (above the gallery) representing Old Testament scenes, the others mainly devoted to scenes from Revelations. Beneath the window is the *Lady Chapel*; on the left *St Stephen's Chapel* with a fine Victorian terracotta Crucifixion in the reredos; on the right *All Saints' Chapel*, the regimental chapel of the Duke of Wellington's Regiment. The *S choir aisle* gives access to the *crypt*, a survival of the earlier Norman church with its splendid Romanesque pillars and vault. Off this aisle, too, is the *Zouche Chapel* (1352) available for private prayer.

During the recent restorations a new *undercroft* was formed by the excavations under the central tower and piers. This is now a *Museum* of relics and church treasures, which include the Horn of Ulf, presented to the Minster by a relative of Canute, a 13th-c. heart casket believed to have belonged to a Crusader, and a collection of plate. There are also the ceremonial cross, ring, cup and plate of the 13th-c.

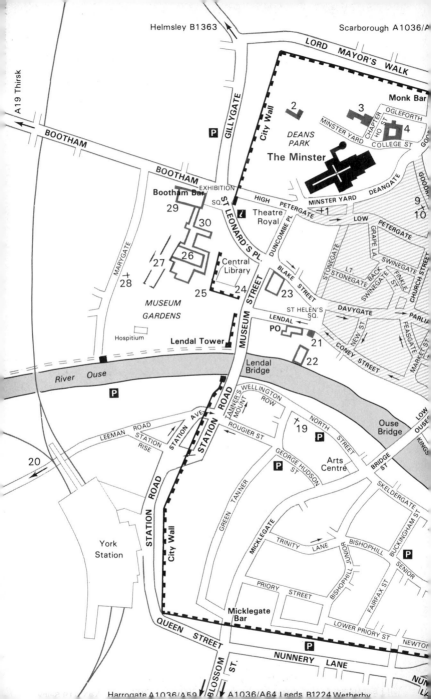

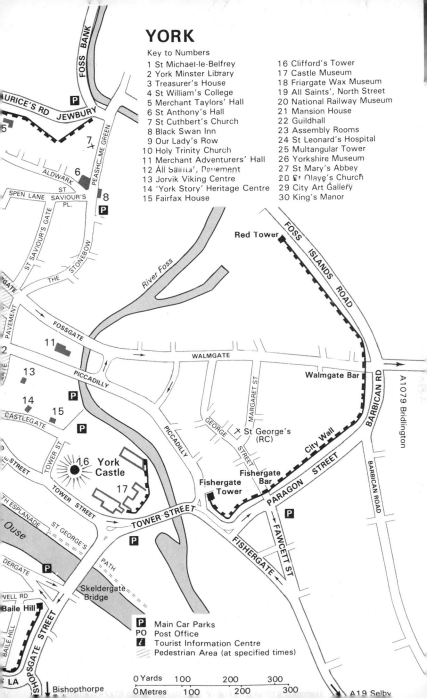

# YORK

Key to Numbers

1 St Michael-le-Belfrey
2 York Minster Library
3 Treasurer's House
4 St William's College
5 Merchant Taylors' Hall
6 St Anthony's Hall
7 St Cuthbert's Church
8 Black Swan Inn
9 Our Lady's Row
10 Holy Trinity Church
11 Merchant Adventurers' Hall
12 All Saints', Pavement
13 Jorvik Viking Centre
14 'York Story' Heritage Centre
15 Fairfax House

16 Clifford's Tower
17 Castle Museum
18 Friargate Wax Museum
19 All Saints', North Street
20 National Railway Museum
21 Mansion House
22 Guildhall
23 Assembly Rooms
24 St Leonard's Hospital
25 Multangular Tower
26 Yorkshire Museum
27 St Mary's Abbey
28 St Olave's Church
29 City Art Gallery
30 King's Manor

**P** Main Car Parks
PO Post Office
*i* Tourist Information Centre
/// Pedestrian Area (at specified times)

0 Yards 100 200 300
0 Metres 100 200 300

Archbishop, Walter de Grey; they were found in his coffin when the tomb was being restored in 1969. Access to the undercroft is from the *S transept*; here, also, is the entrance to the *Central Tower*. On the W side of the transept is *St George's Chapel*, dedicated to the Prince of Wales's Own Regiment (West Yorkshire).

Leaving the Minster by the W door (or S transept door when this is reopened) note, opposite the S side, the restored *column* from the HQ of the Roman 6th Legion. Also S of the Minster is the **Church of St Michael-le-Belfrey**. Built *c.* 1536, the church contains fine 14th- and 16th-c. glass and 17th-c. brasses. Guy Fawkes was baptised here in 1570: the entry in the register can be seen in the Minster Library.

Passing round the W front of the Minster, a gateway leads into the quiet backwater of *Dean's Park*, on the N side. The green is bordered by a section of the arcade of the *cloister* of the Norman Archbishop's Palace and at the E end the *York Minster Library*, which occupies the 13th-c. *chapel* of the palace.

In Chapter House Street off Minster Yard is the **Treasurer's House** (NT), a fine 17th-c. town house with a small formal garden. It stands on the site of the residence of the Minster's treasurer from the Conquest to the Dissolution, and fine furniture and paintings are on display in the rooms open to the public. An exhibition and audio-visual show in the basement illustrates some of the personalities and traditions with which the house is associated. Close by in College Street is the picturesque half-timbered front, with carved oriel windows, of **St William's College**, built in 1465-7 for Minster Chantry priests. During Charles I's sojourn in the city the building served as the king's printing press and Royal Mint. A passage leads through to an attractive courtyard with a projecting upper storey: there are delightful carved wooden figures on the overhang. The college houses the offices of York Minster and the *York Brass Rubbing Centre*.

College Street joins the bustling curve of Goodramgate, which incorporates, or is neighboured by, many medieval buildings. At its N end is *Monk Bar*, with access to the wall-walk (see below); in Aldwark nearby is the 14th-c. **Merchant Taylors' Hall**. (A diversion down Aldwark to Peasholme Green leads to three more historic buildings: on the corner the 15th-c. **St Anthony's Hall**, former home of the guild of that name, further up *St Cuthbert's Church*, the administrative centre for St Michael-le-Belfrey, and opposite, the 16th-c. timber-framed *Black Swan Inn*.)

At the S end of Goodramgate is *Our Lady's Row* (right side) whose houses (1316) are the oldest in the city. Immediately on the right is the entrance gate to **Holy Trinity Church**. This is one of York's oldest and architecturally most interesting churches. Built in the 13th-14th c., the church is predominantly in the Decorated style. The woodwork is later: note the 17th-c. altar rail and 18th-c. wooden box pews. The 15th-c. E window is particularly fine. The tower has a saddle-back (pitched roof) rarely seen in English churches.

At the junction of Goodramgate and Low Petergate is King's Square: here is a tablet recording the building in 107 of the SE gate of the Roman fortress under Trajan. Leading out of the square is the **Shambles**, originally a street of butchers (some of the old meat hooks can still be seen on the buildings). The street is so narrow that the upper storeys of the shops almost touch each other; it gives a fine impression of what a medieval street must have looked like. At *No 35* is the Shrine of the Roman Catholic martyr, St Margaret Clitherow.

The Shambles leads on to Pavement, with (opposite) Fossgate. On the right in Fossgate is the 14th-c. **Merchant Adventurers' Hall**, comprising a great hall, chapel and undercroft. The hall contains portraits of governors and benefactors and the banners of medieval guilds. The oak pillars, roof trusses and beams are a splendid feature, both of the hall and the undercroft. The Adven-

*St William's College*

turers controlled the city's foreign trade for six centuries and was the wealthiest and most powerful of the guilds.

Returning to Pavement, continue S to *All Saints' Church, Pavement*, between High Ousegate and Coppergate. The 15th-c. church has a 19th-c. reproduction of its original octagonal lantern tower, whose light is said to have guided travellers through the forests and marshes to the city – the old lenses are preserved in the church. On the S wall are the shields of the city guilds, which hold their annual services in the church.

From Pavement, proceed along Coppergate. On the left a pedestrian walk leads down to St Mary's Square and the **Jorvik Viking Centre**, an entertaining and highly original reconstruction of Viking York. Between 1976-81, members of the York Archaeological Trust excavated part of the Viking settlement lying beneath the new Coppergate development. Now the knowledge gained from their excavations, and the many relics uncovered, have been utilized in the creation of the Centre. Special 'time cars' enable visitors to travel back in time to the 10th c. through reconstructed streets of the Viking city. In addition, two rows of buildings are preserved just as the archaeologists discovered them, and there is a gallery of the artefacts of the Viking city. Following the square round to Castlegate, the next point of interest is *St Mary's Church* (13th-15th-c.) with its graceful spire. This is now the York Heritage Centre, with a comprehensive and fascinating display of 1000 years of the city's history – **The York Story**.

Turning left down Castlegate, there are two fine Georgian buildings by the York architect John Carr. On the right is *Castlegate House* and on the left **Fairfax House**, open to the public. Completed in 1762 and restored in 1982-3 by the York Civic Trust, the house was built as a residence for Charles Gregory, 9th and last Viscount Fairfax of Emley, and now has on display the magnificent Noel Terry mid-18th-c. collection of furniture and clocks which complements superbly John Carr's elegant concept of an 18th-c. town house.

To the S of Castlegate is **Clifford's Tower**, the keep, and only surviving part, of the old York Castle. Originally it was one of the two timber fortresses built in York by the Normans: the artificial mound on which it stands was formerly surrounded by a moat, crossed by a bridge from the castle courtyard. Destroyed in 1190 when 150 Jews were trapped here and killed during anti-Jewish riots, the tower was rebuilt in stone in 1245-62. It was damaged during the Civil War, and again by an explosion in 1684. From the top there is a splendid view; a surviving part of the interior is the chapel above the gateway.

Across the road to the right is the *Crown Court* building, designed by John Carr (1773-7). The other two buildings on the S and W sides of the circular green known as the 'Eye of York' are the old debtors' prison (1705, centre) and the female prison (1780, left, also the work of Carr) which now form the renowned **Castle Museum**. The founder, Dr J.L. Kirk of Pickering, realised some 80 years ago that everyday objects used by country people in their homes, work and play were rapidly disappearing in the face of mass production and mechanization: from this grew his idea to collect all these objects and bequeath them to the city. The remarkable collection has been augmented over the years, and to see it all adequately requires a tour of at least two hours. There are displays of costumes, militaria, toys, early crafts and domestic and agricultural implements. These complement the period rooms and workshops, Victorian and Edwardian 'streets', the waterpowered corn mill, and a police station and condemned cell – the latter retaining even the graffiti carved by the prisoners. Dick Turpin spent his last night here before his execution. (The highwayman's grave lies to the E of the museum across the River Foss in St George's Churchyard, George Street.) At Christmas the Museum's 'streets' are particularly attractive when it is 'snowing' and carol singers and passers-by appear dressed in period costume.

*St Mary's Abbey*

Returning N towards the city centre by Clifford Street, turn left into Lower Friargate. Here is the **Friargate Wax Museum**, which combines a range of familiar historical figures displayed in tableaux form with the essential 'horror' exhibits. Continuing N to Low Ousegate, the river should now be crossed. At the corner of North Street, the redundant *St John's Church*, Micklegate, is now the *York Arts Centre*. Further along North Street, on the left, is the 12th-15th-c. **All Saints' Church** with its world-famous medieval stained glass: in the NE window are scenes from the life of the Virgin Mary, in the N aisle the Last Fifteen Days and Seven Corporal Acts of Mercy. In the sanctuary is St Anne teaching the child Virgin to read.

Continuing N past Lendal Bridge, proceed through the city walls and along Leeman Road to the **National Railway Museum**, with its collections illustrating the history and develop-

their term of office. The city's regalia, insignia and plate are kept here and can be viewed by appointment. Reached by an arched passage to the right of the Mansion House is the **Guildhall**. Almost totally destroyed by fire during an air raid in 1942, it has been beautifully restored. Particularly noteworthy are the colourful bosses and grotesques of the timber roof, the columns cut from solid oak trunks, the window over the dais which relates the city's story, the wrought-iron balustrade given by York's twin city Münster, and the bronze plaque, dated 1924, expressing felicitations from New York.

In Blake Street, leading out of St Helen's Square, are the **Assembly Rooms**, built by the Earl of Burlington in 1731-2 and restored in 1951. This was the fashionable centre of activity when York was the social capital of the north in Georgian times. The *Central Hall*, supported by 52 Corinthian columns, is in the style of the Egyptian Hall of London's Mansion House. A mural in the *Rotunda* shows Constantine's entry into Roman York: his features are those of the building's architect, Lord Burlington.

At the top of Blake Street turn left into Museum Street. Here is York's *Central Library*, standing in the midst of one of the city's major archaeological areas. Behind the building parts of the Roman and medieval city are exposed, close to a surviving section of the old city wall. To the left of the Library are ruins of the chapel, crypt and ambulatory of the 12th-c. *St Leonard's Hospital*. Further along Museum Street is the entrance to the **Museum Gardens**, the former grounds of St Mary's Abbey. On the right is a section of the old Roman wall with the part-Roman, part-medieval *Multangular Tower* at the corner. To the W is the **Yorkshire Museum** with its archaeological, geological and natural history collections, and beyond, the ruins of **St Mary's Abbey**. Founded in 1089 for the Benedictines, the abbey's most conspicuous ruin is the 13th-c. *Abbey Church* (N wall of nave, part of W

ment of British Railway engineering. Amongst a multitude of exhibits are royal saloons of different reigns, a royal dining car, a travelling post office, some 50 locomotives and items of rolling stock, and George Stephenson's iron bridge which spanned the River Gaunless and was the first structure of its kind in the world. In York Railway Station railways on a different scale feature in *Rail Riders World*, an elaborate model railway layout.

Crossing Lendal Bridge into Museum Street, first right is Lendal, with (left) the *Judges' Lodging*, an imposing building by William Kent (1720), formerly the residence of the Judges of Assize on their visits to York and now a residential hotel. Entering *St Helen's Square*, site of the Praetorian (main) gate to Roman York, the splendid **Mansion House** is on the right. Built in 1725-6, the house has a magnificent stateroom and is the private home of the Lord Mayor and his Lady during front). Down by the river are the *Hospitium* where the abbot entertained (now a storehouse for antiquities) and adjoining *watergate*. Best preserved is the *Gatehouse* by Marygate. Next to it is *St Olave's Church* (18th-c., but founded 11th-c.) whose churchyard, abutting the abbey church ruin, has the grave of the York painter William Etty (1787-1849).

Marygate can be followed right to Bootham, a street with 17th- and 18th-c. *Almshouses* and splendid Georgian houses. At No 51 is *Bootham School*; further up the famous *St Peter's School*. Turning right towards *Bootham Bar* (see below) Exhibition Square is reached on the right, with the **City Art Gallery**. Collections here include Old Masters and the British School, in which William Etty is represented. To the left of the gallery is the historic **King's Manor**, now a hall of residence of the University but formerly the home of the Abbot of St Mary's Abbey. After the Dissolution it became the headquarters of the Council of the North and Henry VIII is thought to have stayed here with Catherine Howard. James VI of Scotland was a guest on his way to London to become James I of England, and Charles I stayed here during the Civil War (the front entrance bears his coat-of-arms).

The 3m-long medieval **city walls** provide an interesting walk with fine views, particularly of the Minster. They are breached at intervals by gateways or '**bars**', most of which have steps allowing access to the walls. Bootham Bar lies to the W of the Minster and then in a clockwise direction are Monk Bar, Walmgate Bar, Fishergate Bar, Victoria Bar (19th-c.) and Micklegate Bar. Of these *Bootham Bar* is the only one that stands on the site of an original Roman gate, the point where the main road (now Bootham) ran N to Scotland. *Monk Bar* is particularly fine, vaulted on three floors and with its portcullis still in working order. *Walmgate Bar* retains its barbican, timber doors, portcullis and Elizabethan house on

top. *Micklegate Bar* was the place where the heads of traitors were displayed.

In addition to the bars there are a number of towers with access to the walls. The main ones are the *Red Tower* and *Fishergate Postern*, at either end of the SE stretch of the wall, and *Baile Hill* on the SW stretch. Across the river from Clifford's Tower, this is the site of William the Conqueror's other castle. In spring the walls walk is particularly attractive when daffodils are in bloom on most parts of the embankment.

Among York's greatest assets are the facilities for eating, drinking and shopping in some of the most attractive streets in the country. There are good cafés, restaurants, inns and hotels, and some splendid shops and galleries, specialities being antiques, crafts, books and fine foods. There is an excellent open-air market off the Shambles (*Newgate Market*). Stonegate and *Coney Street* might be considered the best shopping streets for visitors, but there are several others.

3m S of York, **Bishopthorpe Palace** stands beside the Ouse and is normally best seen from the river (cruises available from city centre) or from the towpath on the opposite bank (a popular walk from York). The gatehouse and stables, however, are seen only from the road in the village. The palace is occasionally open to the public for charity events. It is the Archbishop of York's home and working headquarters and dates from the 13th c., though largely rebuilt in the 18th c.

On the S outskirts of the city in Imphal Barracks, Fulford Road, is the **Regimental Museum of the West Yorkshire Regiment** (Prince of Wales's Own Regiment of Yorkshire).

The **Yorkshire Museum of Farming**, 3m E of the city at Murton, provides fascinating glimpses of the sights and sounds of the countryside in all seasons, with animals, birds, machinery and demonstrations of country crafts and activities. A section of the old Derwent Valley Railway is maintained with its rolling stock. The James Herriot Surgery is another special feature.

*York city wall and Minster*

# Gazetteer

EC: Early closing   MD: Market Day
Populations over 10,000 shown

Map references after place names
refer to map inside back cover

Information centres quoted offer a
tourist accommodation booking service

Note: Many of these offices in the
smaller towns are closed in winter

**This includes information
on the location, history and
main features of the places
of interest in the region.
Visiting hours for all places
open to the public are shown
in 'The Best of the Region'.
Asterisks indicate references
to other Gazetteer entries.
(NT) indicates properties
owned by the National Trust;
(FC) Forestry Commission**

While defining the area covered by this guide for
practical purposes as the county of North
Yorkshire, we have taken excursions outside the
area for some places of interest within easy reach,
crossing into the county of Cleveland for
Guisborough Priory, the county of West Yorkshire
for Haworth (Brontë Parsonage) and into the
county of Humberside for the resorts of Filey and
Bridlington, the great natural features of
Flamborough Head and Bempton Cliffs, and the
historic houses of Sledmere and Burton Agnes.

## Airedale & Malhamdale
A3

*N Yorks. Dales in Yorkshire Dales National Park*

81m long, the River Aire drains an area of 423
sq m from its source on Malham Moor to its
confluence with the Ouse at Airmyn in
Humberside. The river rises deep
underground in the limestone above Malham
Tarn, between Wharfedale and Ribblesdale
in the *Craven* district, and is not visible until
it leaves the tarn. It again disappears before
finally emerging above *Malham*, at the foot
of Malham Cove.

Flowing at the outset through Malhamdale
in some of the wildest limestone fell and
moorland scenery of the *Yorkshire Dales
National Park*, the Aire meanders through
gentler Airedale countryside from Gargrave
to Skipton. Thence it flows S to industrial
West Yorkshire.

*Gargrave*, gateway to Malhamdale,
occupies the *Aire Gap* which separates the
Southern from the Central Pennines and is
part of the complex series of Craven Faults.
The Gap is the only thoroughfare across the
Pennines which reaches no higher than 500ft:
the Skipton-Lake District road crosses here,
as well as the *Leeds-Liverpool Canal*.

Although most of Airedale has industrial
surroundings it also has important tourist
sites, notably the Brontë sisters' home at
*Haworth* in the valley of the River Worth,
near Keighley (see *Skipton*).

The *Pennine Way* enters Malhamdale at
Gargrave, and follows the river to its source.

## Aldborough
B3

*N Yorks. Village off B6265, 8m SE of Ripon*

Aldborough is the last village beside the Ure
before the river joins the Swale to form the
Ouse. It is an attractive place with an ancient
cross and stocks, and a maypole on a spacious
green. White-washed cottages mix with
Georgian-style houses and the 14th-c. *St
Andrew's Church*.

The site of the village was the Roman town
of Isurium, which may have developed from
a stronghold of Cartimandua, Queen of the
Brigantes, who betrayed Caractacus to the
Roman invaders. Covering some 60 acres,
Isurium Brigantum was a flourishing river
port; the remains of foundations, walls and
mosaic pavements are evidence of its
importance, and some of these can be seen *in
situ*. Hundreds of artefacts used by the
inhabitants in their work and social activities,
including pottery, tiles and glass, are on
display in the **Museum**, and a stone panel can
be seen in the village church. Aldborough
declined in Norman times, when a bridge
was built 1m upstream at *Boroughbridge*.

## Ampleforth Abbey and College    C2

*Ryedale. Off A170, 3m SW of Helmsley*

By normal abbey standards Ampleforth is a modern creation, dating from 1802 when a group of Benedictine monks fled here in the aftermath of the French Revolution. In a sense it was a homecoming for the Order, which had moved to France after the Dissolution of Westminster Abbey. In the last 180 years the College has become one of the principal Roman Catholic schools in the country, renowned for its academic and sporting attainments.

The **Abbey Church of St Laurence** was designed by Sir Giles Gilbert Scott, and took 40 years to complete (1960). Probably the most unusual feature is the position of the high altar and choir in the W transept. The stone altar piers and their arch are carved with figures of bishops, saints and angels; the oak choir stalls, lectern and screen are outstanding examples of the work of the wood-carver Robert Thompson, from *Kilburn*. The three-light window has beautiful modern stained glass with representations of the life of Christ from the Annunciation to the Ascension. The sanctuary occupies the space beneath the 120ft-high central tower; there are four chapels on the S side and 25 more in the crypt, with fine wood and stone carvings.

The Cardinal Archbishop of Westminster, Basil Hume, was formerly Abbot and Head-master. Visitors to the abbey are welcome, but the College is open to the public only on written application to the Guestmaster.

Ampleforth stands at the S edge of the Hambleton Hills; SE across the valley of the Holbeck, which runs E to join the River Rye, stands the fine castle at *Gilling East* (acquired by the College for its Junior School in 1930) with the Howardian Hills beyond.

## Appletreewick    A3

*Wharfedale. Village off B6160, 4m SE of Grassington*

A single-street village, with its houses straggling along both sides for a considerable distance. Close by is the Elizabethan *Parceval Hall*, restored some 50 years ago. Now in the possession of the Bradford Diocese, it is used as a Church of England conference centre and retreat. The **Grounds**, with views and walks, are open to the public. John Nevison the highwayman, who was hanged at York after a long career of murder and robbery, is said to have used the Hall as a refuge. Nearby is *Trollers Gill*, a ½m long limestone gorge. In more fanciful times it was believed to be the lair of the Barguest, a spectral hound with saucer-sized eyes.

The river close to Appletreewick is well known for its white water, and canoeing championships are held here from time to time. 1m downstream is 17th-c. *Woodside Manor*, birthplace of Nelson's maternal grandmother. The minor road follows the E bank of the Wharfe upstream towards *Hebden*, an old village on the Grassington-Pateley Bridge road. (See also *Walks*, p. 23.)

## Arncliffe    A3

*Wharfedale (Littondale). Village off B6160, 11m NE of Settle*

The church, houses and inn of this pretty place cluster round a green on the banks of the River Skirfare, a little tributary of the Wharfe which it joins between Kettlewell and Kilnsey. Beyond Arncliffe, *Littondale* is set in wild and majestic hill scenery with many small tributary dales cut through the limestone uplands which stretch between here and the Craven area around Settle.

Charles Kingsley used to stay here, at *Bridge End*, with the Hammond family. Inspired by the house, its mistress and the river, he included them in early chapters of *The Water Babies*, and called the valley 'Vendale'.

Hang-gliding takes place on the fells downstream, and botanists are rewarded by a variety of wild flowers which flourish on the limestone. Specialities are mountain avens, bird's eye primrose and lily-of-the-valley.

## Askrigg    A2

*Wensleydale. Village off A684, 4m W of Aysgarth*

Askrigg, with its old inns and Georgian houses, was once a busy market and coaching centre; trading later spread to Hawes up-river and to Leyburn downstream. At one time the village was a clock-making centre, and renowned for its hand-knitting trade, but now its economy relies on agriculture and tourism. A sad relic of bull-baiting days is an iron *bullring* set in the cobble-stoned market place outside the 15th-c. church, *St Oswald's*.

The church, with its fine nave roof, has a memorial to Leonard Wilson, former Bishop of Birmingham, who was taken prisoner by the Japanese in World War II and became well known for defiance of his captors and for the encouragement he gave to fellow prisoners. Askrigg is the home of the well-known authors Joan Ingilby and Marie Hartley, prolific writers on the Dales.

From near the church a walk to the 70ft-high *Mill Gill Force* is rewarding: here Cogill Beck plunges down a flight of limestone steps in a wooded and rocky glen. Further up is *Whitfield Gill Force*.

Askrigg stands at a meeting of moorland roads on the N side of the Ure. Near the road following the dale, a mile or so toward Carperby (E), is the castellated *Nappa Hall*, now a farmhouse, with panoramic dale views. Other roads climb steeply N of the village and cross the moors to Swaledale.

## Aysgarth A2
*Wensleydale. Village on A684, 9m E of Hawes. Nat Park Inf: Tel (09693) 424*

Aysgarth is perhaps the most visited part of upper Wensleydale because of the famous **Aysgarth Falls**, which are particularly spectacular when the river is in spate, leaping and roaring over the rocks between its wooded banks.

Aysgarth stands on the main road S of the river. Near the bottom of the steep hill down to the river, **St Andrew's Church** stands high above the water and within sight and sound of the falls. In spite of being rebuilt in 1866, the Church has some interesting features, notably a carved rood screen dating from about 1500, one of the finest in the county, and a lectern made from poppy-headed pew-ends. Both are thought to be the work of the Ripon Carvers for Coverham Abbey near *East Witton*.

Immediately below the church, in a disused flour mill, is the **Yorkshire Museum of Carriages and Horse-Drawn Vehicles**. The mill is contiguous with the 16th-c. single-arched bridge across the Ure, a good viewpoint for the *Upper Falls*, which are within easy walking distance. From this point the generally placid river becomes a foaming torrent; the cataracts and falls extend for a distance of ½m or more, the most spectacular being the *Lower Falls*.

Between the church and the village, a precipitous road descends S to meet *Bishopdale*.This broad fertile tributary dale carries the B6160 SW over Kidstones Pass, 1392ft, to Wharfedale. A quiet neighbouring dale, *Walden Dale*, with Buckden Pike at its head, can be explored by minor roads leading from West Burton: these are more suited to walkers than to motorists.

## Bainbridge A2
*Wensleydale. Village on A684, 4m E of Hawes. EC Wed*

Built around a large green on rising ground above the river, this delightful village stands at a Roman crossing point near the remains of a 1st-c. *fort* which occupies Brough Hill (E). On the green are the stocks and a couple of millstones, and just above the bridge (which was widened in 1785 by the York architect John Carr) is *Bain Fall*, a crescent-shaped

waterfall cascading over a limestone bed. N of the village the Bain joins the Ure.

The Bainbridge horn tradition originated in Norman times when the surrounding countryside was thickly forested, and it was customary to blow the horn to guide travellers to the safety of the village. The ceremony is still re-enacted in the autumn and winter from Hawes Back-End Fair, or Holyrood (late September), until Shrove Tuesday. Standing on the village green, the hornblower gives three long blasts on an instrument first used in 1864. The horn, when not in use, can be seen in *The Rose and Crown* inn. An older horn is preserved in *Bolton Castle* (9m E); a similar but better-known ceremony takes place nightly at *Ripon*.

S of Bainbridge, along either side of the Bain valley, minor roads lead to *Semerwater* (2m), a small lake now used for yachting and water skiing. From a little way along the W road can be followed the route of a Roman road which lead SW across the Pennine moors; the *Pennine Way*, crossing Cam Fell from Ribblesdale (S) to *Hawes*, follows part of this route. This is ideal fell-walking country.

## Barden Tower A3
*Wharfedale. On B6160, 9m NE of Skipton*

Barden Tower stands beside the single-track, buttressed and humpbacked *Barden Bridge*, which has only the Old Bridge at Ilkley as a rival for attractiveness and charm. Henry, Lord Clifford, built the tower as a hunting lodge in 1485 when the Clifford lands were restored to the family after being forfeit to the Crown at the Yorkist victory in the Wars of the Roses.

Lord Clifford was known as the 'Shepherd Lord' because his mother feared for his life at the hands of the Yorkists, and he was brought up in obscurity as a minder of sheep. The tower fell into ruin, but was restored by Lady Anne Clifford in 1657 and remained intact until the end of the 18th c. Part of today's ruin serves as a café during the tourist season.

## Beck Hole see *Goathland*

## Bedale B2
*N Yorks. Town on A684/B6285/B6268, 9m SW of Northallerton. EC Thur MD Tue*

This quaint little town stands on Bedale Beck, and in spite of its position at a triple junction close to the A1 it retains an old-world charm in the haphazard arrangement of its houses, shops and cobbled market place.

The market place, which has a 14th-c. *cross* atop a flight of steps, narrows into the main street and slopes upward, N, to Bedale Hall and **St Gregory's Church**. The tower of the church dates from the 14th c. and is believed to have been erected as a refuge from Scottish invaders; evidence suggests that access to a first floor room was safeguarded by a portcullis. The S porch, which is attached to the tower, has tunnel vaulting. The nave is wide, with early 13th-c. arcading, and the chancel roof rests on figures of angels. Under the sanctuary a stairway leads to a vaulted crypt. 14th-c. wall paintings in the nave include a restored St George and the Dragon, while 20th-c. work includes a reredos with saints in niches, and an oak pulpit with scenes from the life of St Gregory.

There is much else to see in this interesting old church before crossing the street to **Bedale Hall**, an early Georgian mansion now occupied by the offices of Hambleton District Council. The *Ballroom* has a superb Italian plasterwork ceiling, and a small **Craft Museum** next-door includes in its exhibits an 18th-c. hand-drawn fire engine, a collection of grandfather clocks and some small farming and tradesmen's tools.

**Bempton Cliffs** D2
*Humberside. Off B1229, 5m N of Bridlington*
These sheer chalk cliffs W of Flamborough Head, rising to 400ft, are topped with boulder clay; ledges and fissures in the softer upper level of the chalk provide nesting sites for many species of seabird, including Britain's only mainland gannet colony. Other species include kittiwakes, fulmars, shags and three kinds of auk: guillemot, razorbill and puffin. Native landbirds and migrating visitors can also be seen.

The Royal Society for the Protection of Birds established its *Bird Reserve* here in 1970, later providing a car park and information point. Along this part of the public footpath which follows the clifftop between *Filey* and Flamborough Head are observation posts.

The centre of the reserve can be reached by car along Cliff Lane from *Bempton* village. *Danes' Dyke*, which cuts 2½m S-N across the neck of Flamborough Head, ends close to the E end of the reserve. A *Nature Trail* can be followed along its length. The best time to visit the reserve, when there is maximum bird activity, is between late May and early July.

The cliffs can be followed SE to *Flamborough Head*, with the best scenery (caves and stacks) E of *North Landing*.

**Beningbrough Hall** (NT) C3
*N Yorks. Historic house off A19, 8m NW of York*
Completed in 1716, this Baroque house is situated at the edge of water meadows on the E bank of the River Ouse. It is built of claret-coloured, crusted brick (made from alluvial clay found on the river's banks), ornamented with dressed stone. On two sides of the entrance courtyard there are small pavilions with cupolas connected to the house by screen walls. The N front is approached along a double avenue of limes leading from the entrance archway, flanked on either side by a small lodge. An American garden and an adventure playground are features of the well laid-out *Grounds*.

The house's outstanding features are its inventive interior wood carving and magnificent, three-flight cantilevered *staircase*, the work of York craftsmen. These attributes are supported by fine furniture, ceramics and Oriental porcelain and, from the National Portrait Gallery, an excellent selection of some 100 portraits featuring personalities of the period 1688-1760. There is a Victorian *Laundry*; and sound and vision displays illustrate domestic life at all levels.

**Bilsdale** C2
*Ryedale. Dale NW of Helmsley*
This remote and sparsely-populated dale is watered by the River Seph which flows close to the B1257 running N-S to *Helmsley* from Stokesley. The road climbs past *Rievaulx Terrace* to *Newgate Bank* in the forest area W of Rievaulx Moor, where the Seph joins the Rye. At the FC car park and picnic place there is a fine view along the dale to the Cleveland Hills. There are also good walks from here along *Roppa Edge* (E), where a controversial aluminium sculpture by Austin Wright has been erected by the Yorkshire Arts Association. From here a gated road runs down to Helmsley Church.

2m N of Newgate Bank is the 16th-17th-c. 'Spout House', of cruck construction with a thatched roof, restored by the North York Moors National Park Committee. Until 1914, when the present *Sun Inn* was built, this old building served as the local hostelry. Further up the dale, at *Beak Hill Farm* beneath Cold Moor, are the kennels of the Bilsdale Hunt; the hounds are descended from those of the Duke of Buckingham who lived at Helmsley Castle in the 17th c.

Along its higher and bleaker stretches, the road crosses close to Urra Moor where *Botton Head* reaches the highest point of the Cleveland Hills at 1490ft. Just before this point, the road is crossed by the *Lyke Wake*

*Walk* and the *\*Cleveland Way*. The Forestry Commission has a picnic place by the B1257 at *Clay Bank* in the Cleveland Forest; there are magnificent views from here over Urra (E) and Hasty Bank (W), and towards Teesside.

**Bolton Abbey**                              A3
*Wharfedale. Village on B6160, 6m NW of Ilkley*
The village is part of the Duke of Devonshire's estate and is famous for the Augustinian **Priory of St Mary and St Cuthbert**, founded in 1154 and known as 'Bolton Abbey'.

The priory stands in ruined splendour on a hillock where the river flows round a huge bend, with pastureland on the W bank and an almost vertical escarpment on the E, complete with waterfall. A timber pedestrian bridge and stepping stones connect the banks. Long before the Dissolution the villagers were permitted to use the priory nave as their church, and this practice still continues: the only building of substance that survives, it incorporates fine examples of work from different medieval periods. The 12th-c. arcades, the Decorated E window and the grandeur of the Perpendicular W front make noble contrast with the homely atmosphere created by the building's continuing use as parish church. The roof and E end were restored in the late 19th c. by G.E. Street.

The priory in its magnificent setting has long attracted artists and photographers, among them the painters Girtin, Turner, Cotman and Landseer. Beside the priory are the *Rectory* and the *Hall*, the Devonshire family's shooting lodge. Both are beautiful and distinguished buildings. Adjoining the Hall, an 18th-c. *archway* spans the road; once an aqueduct for a mill, it now imposes a single-line traffic restriction.

Upstream, at an entrance to Bolton Woods, is the **Cavendish Memorial**. This imposing structure takes the form of a fountain and commemorates Lord Frederick Cavendish, appointed Chief Secretary for Ireland and murdered with his deputy by 'Irish Invincibles' in Phoenix Park, Dublin (1882).

Flowing through beautiful *Bolton Woods* between Barden Tower and Bolton Abbey, the river takes on a sinister aspect as its waters are compressed into a narrow defile in the millstone grit, only a few feet wide. The **Strid** is over 30ft deep, and the fast-flowing water has scooped out large hollows in the steeply undercut, rocky sides, so that any object falling in can be held tightly by water

pressure. The distance across seems safe enough, but the rocks are slippery and leaping the gap is dangerous.

A tragedy is said to have occurred here in the mid 12th c. when the son of Alicia de Romilly, the Priory's founder, was out in the woods with his greyhound. Immortalised in Wordsworth's poem *The Force of Prayer*, the 'Boy of Egremont' attempted to leap across, but was thrown into the water and drowned when his dog tried to hold him back. Many others have met the same fate, and the Strid is just as perilous today.

An excellent walking route follows a narrow road along the river's E bank between Bolton Abbey and *\*Barden Tower*. Passing Forestry Commission plantations and an ancient oak so old that it needs support, the route passes through part of Bolton Woods and across a ford, which is set in a little valley almost opposite the wooden bridge crossing the river to the *Cavendish Pavilion*. This refreshment place is the start of the walk upstream to the Strid. Not far from the venerable oak, a path leads to the *Valley of Desolation* and the moors beyond. The valley gets its name from the havoc resulting from the tremendous storm of 1826. Another fine walk from here takes visitors up to *Simon Seat*, a crag on the moors with panoramic views from its summit of 1592ft.

*The Craven Heifer* is a name associated with public houses in Airedale and Wharfedale. They are so named because of a giant cow bred in 1897 by the Rev William Carr, rector of the Priory Church for 54 years. The animal weighed just short of two tons, had a shoulder height of 5ft 2in, was 11ft 2in long, had a middle girth of 10ft 2in and a loin girth of 9ft 11in.

**Bolton Castle**                              A2
*Wensleydale. Off A684, 5m NE of Aysgarth*
Built around a courtyard and entered through an arched gateway, this massive and brooding castle was erected at the end of the 14th c. by Sir Richard Scrope, a survivor of the Battle of Crécy and Richard II's Lord Chancellor. The castle occupies a commanding position above the River Ure, and looks across at the equally forbidding *Penhill* to the S.

A minor road leading from Wensley along the dale's N edge passes through the nearby village of *Redmire*, and a side road further up the dale leads to the village of *Castle Bolton* and the castle. Designed to serve also as a dwelling, the castle is noted for its combination of comparative domestic comfort with military might. Four huge towers stood at the corners of a domestic range which formed the side of a square interior courtyard; the interior is ruinous, but the exterior (except for one tower destroyed in a storm) is remarkably complete.

The basement accommodated the stables, armoury, kitchens, dungeon and well, while on the upper floors were a chapel and priests' rooms, and a banqueting hall which now serves as a **Dales Museum**. Amongst other artefacts displayed here is an Armada treasure chest; an ancient *Bainbridge* horn can also be seen. The castle has a licensed restaurant.

This was the second place of imprisonment for Mary, Queen of Scots after she fled to England from Scotland. She arrived from Carlisle in July 1568 and was confined in one of the towers for six months before being moved to Tutbury. During her time here, it is said, she attempted is escape and was recaptured near *Leyburn* (5m E). During the Civil War, the castle held out for a year under the Royalist command of John Scrope before falling to Cromwell's troops.

The early 15th-c. St Oswald's Church lies behind the castle, and in Castle Bolton attractive old cottages sit back from the road behind wide grass verges. The moors between here and Swaledale (N) are strewn with disused mineworkings; *Redmire* and other villages nearby were the homes of leadminers in the 19th c.

**Bolton-on-Swale** B2
*N Yorks. Village on B6271, 5m E of Richmond*
Village and church stand on Scorton Beck about ½m E of, and across the road from the River Swale. **St Mary's** has an unusual *N chapel* embellished with sculpted friezes of men at work in cornfield and woodland, and of a sailing ship entering port. There is also a medallion of Christ subduing the waves and, in the centre of the chapel, a white marble pedestal supporting a woman's head and shoulders lying on a pillow.

Other interesting memorials include an *obelisk* in the churchyard commemorating Henry Jenkins who, as a boy of 12 years, carted arrows to the Battle of Flodden (1513). The task apparently did him little harm, as his memorial slab in the church tells us he lived to be 169.

2m SE of the village is **Kiplin Hall**, a pretty red-brick gabled mansion with domed towers designed in the 1620s by Inigo Jones for the 1st Lord Baltimore. His son Cecil, the 2nd Baron, was granted the instrument which led to the founding of Maryland, with Baltimore as its capital. The new state was named after

Charles I's queen, Henrietta Maria, and its first governor was Cecil's younger brother, Leonard. Nelson's sister-in-law, Lady Tyrconnel, lived here. The *Grounds* have lakes, vineries and orchards.

**Boroughbridge** B3
*N Yorks. Town on B6265 (A1), 7m SE of Ripon. EC Thur MD Mon, Tue. Inf: Tel (09012) 2876*
For nine centuries Boroughbridge has stood at a main crossing point over the River Ure, which here tumbles over a weir and salmon ladder near a handsome triple-arched *bridge*. After the first bridge was built by the Normans, the town's importance grew while its busier neighbour downstream, the former Romano-British settlement at *Aldborough*, declined.

Now bypassed by the main road, Boroughbridge with its coaching inns and Regency, Georgian and Victorian buildings retains an old-world atmosphere. In cobbled St James's Square, an artesian well is covered by a cupola-topped canopy supported on columns. *St James's Church* has an arched late Norman doorway, decorated with figures and foliage.

Three enormous millstone-grit monoliths, believed to be of the Bronze Age and known as the **Devil's Arrows**, stand in a field to the W. 16ft in girth and 24ft above ground, they are among Yorkshire's best-known prehistoric monuments.

**Braithwaite Hall** see *East Witton*

**Bransdale** (NT) C2
*Ryedale. Dale on Hodge Beck NE of Helmsley*
Rising on the S edge of the *North Yorkshire Moors* and fed by numerous streams, *Hodge Beck* drains the beautiful landlocked valley of Bransdale, cutting deeply through the limestone on its way S. As it approaches the Vale of Pickering the broadening beck flows through *Kirk Dale* (see *Kirkbymoorside*).

No road runs through these dales, but a minor road from *Helmsley* leads N past the *Cow House Bank* picnic site, with a fine view S along *Riccal Dale*, then crosses the lonely Helmsley Moor to skirt Bransdale's W flank, rounding the dale head at *Cockayne*. Returning E of Bransdale, the road leads between Kirk Dale and *Farndale* to *Gillamoor*, arriving finally at the town of Kirkbymoorside overlooking the Vale of Pickering.

The National Trust, which owns much of Bransdale, is restoring an old *Mill* at Cockayne.

**Bridestones** see *Thornton Dale*

## Bridlington D3

*Humberside. Pop 26,920. 11m SE of Filey (A165/A166). Events: East Coast Vintage & Veteran Vehicle Rally (2nd Sun in Jun); Dance Festival (Jul); RYYC Regatta (Aug); Angling Festival (Sep). EC Thur MD Wed, Sat. Inf: Tel (0262) 673474/678255*

Sheltered on the NE by *Flamborough Head*, Bridlington stands N of the huge sweep of Bridlington Bay, a good haven for shipping in storms. The town is a popular resort offering all the usual amenities, and attracts many thousands of visitors each year; some prefer its flat, accessible coastline to that of its rivals situated on the sides and tops of cliffs higher up the coast.

The harbour, protected by two piers built with stones from the old priory, is a hive of activity as yachts and other craft ply in and out of the bay. Local fishermen and anglers are kept busy here, and their wares can be sampled at the numerous seafood stalls on the harbourside. Fine long sands stretch N and S. Vestiges of the old fishing town can be seen here, with 17th-c. houses and old inns near the waterside. In Harbour Road the **Harbour and History Museum** has aquaria, dioramas and marine displays.

On the sea front are the huge glass *Floral Pavilion*, the *Spa Theatre* and the *Royal Hall* which cater for all the seaside entertainments; nearby are the swimming pool and solarium, and the inevitable amusement arcades. In the *South Cliff Gardens* a sundial commemorates Lawrence of Arabia who, as Aircraftsman Shaw, was based here with the RAF air-sea rescue service in the 1930s.

**St Mary's Church** was founded in 1114 as an Augustinian priory, and considerably restored in the late 19th c. It is worth walking the mile inshore to see the church's cathedral-like proportions and fine features, particularly the N porch, W doorway and huge W window. Notable features of the interior are the 14th-c. S aisle and Caen stone reredos. The late 14th-c. Priory Gatehouse, now called the **Bayle Gate**, houses a museum.

Bridlington's other architectural attraction (2m N) is in *Sewerby Park* with its golf course, *Gardens*, woodlands and small *Zoo*. The early 18th-c. *Hall* is used as an **Art Gallery and Museum**, and has a room with displays commemorating the pioneer airwoman Amy Johnson, born in Hull. There is also a restaurant.

Sewerby marks the S end of the 2½m *Danes' Dyke* which stretches across the neck of *Flamborough Head*. Inland, to the W of Bridlington, lies the hilly rural countryside of the Yorkshire Wolds.

## Brimham Rocks (NT) B3

*Nidderdale. Off B6165 & B6265, 8m SW of Ripon. Nat Trust Inf: Tel (0423) 780688*

Covering an area of some 60 acres E of *Pateley Bridge*, this extraordinary series of millstone grit outcrops, contorted into grotesque and striking shapes by the passage of ice floes, time and weather, was thrown up by a gigantic upheaval in the Carboniferous period. The rocks are surrounded by a carpet of bracken and heather reaching nearly 1000ft above sea-level and affording a tremendous panorama across Nidderdale and the Plain of York to the hills beyond, with the city's great Minster clearly visible in the distance.

Some of the major formations weigh hundreds of tons; their shapes have given them fanciful names varying from 'Pulpit' or 'Druid's Writing Desk' to 'Oyster Shell', 'Dancing Bear', 'Baboon'. The National Trust has an Information Centre at *Brimham House*, near the rocks.

## Brompton see *Scarborough*

## Buckden A2

*Wharfedale. Village on B6160, 17m N of Skipton*

Of recent years the village has become established as a holiday centre with cafés, hotels and cottages to let. However, it still manages to retain the charm of not so long ago, when it was largely the preserve of cyclists and hikers. There is a stiff climb up to *Buckden Pike*, which offers a magnificent panorama encompassing the Irish Sea 36m W, and the North Sea at Teesmouth 46m NE.

## Burnsall A3

*Wharfedale. Village on B6160, 11m NE of Skipton. EC Mon, Thur. Event: Feast Day (Aug). Inf: Tel (075672) 295*

This delightfully situated village has a green and maypole close to the bridge over the River Wharfe. Its church, *St Wilfrid's*, is approached by a lych-gate and was last remodelled in 1612. Among its more interesting objects are two hogsback tombstones, a Norman font and a 13th-c. alabaster carving of the Adoration of the Magi.

In this part of Wharfedale the river is particularly beautiful, a limpid placid stretch flowing past the village after a turbulent reach ½m upstream at *Loop Scar*. Here it traverses a faulting in the limestone, the water having gouged out a channel in the form of an S-bend.

The fells rising steeply to the SW of the village are the scene, each August, of a Feast Day race starting and finishing on the green.

*Bolton Priory*

*Robin Hood's Bay*

Other events include canoe races and pillow fights. There are fine views of the village from the top of the hill on the Ilkley road.

### Burton Agnes Hall                              D3
*Humberside. Historic house on A166, 6m SW of Bridlington*

Based on a Norman manor, this beautiful early 17th-c. house stands basically unaltered, with its village, at the edge of the Yorkshire Wolds, overlooking the flat fertile farmlands of the Plain of Holderness.

A *Topiary Garden* separates the grand *Gatehouse* from the Hall, whose original interiors include a fine oak staircase, chimney-pieces carved in oak, stone and alabaster, and ornate plasterwork ceilings; French 19th and early 20th-c. paintings hang on the walls. Also noteworthy is the *Long Gallery*, perfectly restored in 1951 after it had served as staff accommodation following the collapse of the ceiling in 1810. The Hall, which is haunted, belongs to descendants of the family who built it (1598-1610).

The village cottages surround a duck pond fringed with trees, and *St Martin's Church* is well-known for its fine yews. It dates from the Norman period.

At the Wolds village of *Rudston*, 4m N on the B1253, a gigantic **monolith** stands in *All Saints'* churchyard. Over 25ft high, it is thought to have been deposited near here by glacial action and erected in prehistoric times; one theory says that the gritstone block was dragged here from the Scarborough area. *Rudston House* in the village was the birthplace of the novelist Winifred Holtby (1898), who was buried in the churchyard after her untimely death in 1935.

The *Gypsey Race*, one of the Wolds' erratically-flowing rivers, flows through the village on its way E to Bridlington from Duggleby, close to Wharram-le-Street (see *\*Sledmere*); in its higher reaches the water appears approximately every five years.

### Buttertubs Pass see *Hawes*

### Byland Abbey                              C2
*Ryedale. Off A170, 6m SW of Helmsley*

Hauntingly set in a wide valley beneath the Hambleton Hills near the small village of *Wass*, this 12th-c. ruin is distinguished by the great half-circle of a *rose window* in its W end and by the lofty N side of its church, which survives among other massive skeletal remains.

The Cistercian abbey was established here in 1177 after various unsatisfactory moves,

following its foundation from Furness Abbey in Cumbria in 1134: a previous location was Old Byland, 5m to the N, which proved to be too near Rievaulx Abbey. The original ground plan can be followed in the ruins, which still retain some of the abbey's fine 13th-c. green-and-yellow tiled floors; most notably in the S transept chapels.

Until the Dissolution the abbey's life was generally tranquil, although the Scots caused much damage in their pursuit of Edward II, who was almost captured while at dinner here with the Abbot during the Battle of Byland (1322). This took place around 'Scotch Corner' on an ancient drovers' route known as Hambleton Drove Road which descends steeply from the Hambleton Hills to the NW.

### Castle Howard                              C3
*N Yorks. Historic house off A64/B1257, 6m W of Malton*

This splendid mansion, the largest house in Yorkshire, was built for the Howard family, the Earls of Carlisle. From York, the house is approached by a minor road which leads through the undulating countryside of the Howardian Hills and thence along a 5m avenue through the *Park*; the turning to the house is marked by a 100ft obelisk. The house faces formal gardens with a magnificent fountain.

Designed by Sir John Vanbrugh with the assistance of Nicholas Hawksmoor, it combines all the grand Classical features associated with the other work of these architects (Hawksmoor's Greenwich Palace, Vanbrugh's Blenheim). Built between 1700-37, the house has a large pedimented central block topped by a cupola with wings on either side. The lantern and dome and part of the S front were destroyed by fire in 1940 but have been skilfully restored.

There are several impressive rooms including the Baroque *Entrance Hall*, 52ft square and 70ft high beneath the finely restored dome, the *Long Gallery* in the W wing, and the *Orleans*, *Music* and *Tapestry Rooms*. The ornate *Chapel* has stained glass by Burne-Jones and William Morris, and a Madonna and Child by Sansovino.

Among Castle Howard's many great works of art are paintings by Holbein, Rubens and Gainsborough. There is furniture by Chippendale, and to designs by Sheraton and Adam, collections of Egyptian and Graeco-Roman antiquities, and china from several famous factories.

The beautifully laid-out *Grounds*, covering 1000 acres, include the *Great Lake* N of the house, and on the S the Temple, Mausoleum and Pyramid. The Ionic portico of Vanbrugh's domed *Temple of the Four Winds* (1724-26) opens on to a floor of Portland stone inlaid with marble. Near a bridge across the New River is the grand **Mausoleum** (1728-29) by Hawksmoor, where the Carlisle family lie buried in the crypt beneath the chapel, and further S on St Anne's Hill is the *Pyramid*, enclosing a large bust of Lord William Howard (d. 1639).

In recent years Castle Howard has featured in several film and television productions, notably *Brideshead Revisited*. The facilities include a cafeteria, licensed restaurant, shop and market garden.

**Castleton**                                    C1
*Esk Dale. Village on minor road 17m W of Whitby*
Castleton stands surrounded by wild moorland in higher *\*Esk Dale*, where Danby Beck flows in from the S to meet the River Esk. A little way further up-dale the river tumbling from its source on Westerdale (S) turns E on its long journey to Whitby on the North Sea.

The few terraces of stone houses follow the direction of the road above the valley; the *castle motte* overlooks the river. Fine moorland scenery can be enjoyed from roads leading S on either side of Castleton Rigg to Ralph Cross at the head of Rosedale, and thence into the dale, or along *Blakey Ridge* (E of Farndale) to Hutton-le-Hole overlooking the Vale of Pickering.

**Ralph Cross**, which is passed by the route of the *\*Lyke Wake Walk*, is one of many well-known stone waymarks originating from medieval times (this one is an 18th-c. replacement). They were also used by travellers as receptacles for alms. Just E of Ralph Cross, on the Rosedale road, is the squat, white cross known as '*Fat Betty*'; its head was once detachable and the alms placed beneath, but recently the head has been cemented in place. The symbol of the North York Moors National Park is taken from Ralph Cross.

**Catterick Bridge**                              B2
*N Yorks. Village on B6136, 3m E of Richmond*
The Roman town of Cataractonium occupied a site close to the 15th-c. four-arched bridge which carries the A1 across the River Swale at Catterick Bridge; the bypass actually cuts through the citadel. A military camp of some consequence in Roman times, the area is still very much an army centre, a huge complex situated between Catterick Bridge and Richmond and appropriately enough called *Catterick Camp*. It is an unsightly sprawl of

modern houses, shops, barracks, schools and recreational centres devoted entirely to the service of the military. The Camp was established during World War I by Earl Kitchener of Khartoum.

1m S of the bridge, *Catterick* village has old houses and coaching inns grouped around its green. In *St Ann's Church*, a Perpendicular building of 1415, is a window showing Paulinus preaching to Edwin, King of Northumbria. Paulinus, who became Bishop of York, spent much time in the area preaching and baptising in the waters of the River Swale. The Northumbrian kings had their palace on **Castle Hill** in a loop of the river 1m SW, where a Norman motte and bailey later stood; its remains reach 60ft in places. In 1816 the Rev Alexander Scott was appointed Vicar of St Ann's. 11 years earlier he had been chaplain on board the *Victory* at the Battle of Trafalgar, and it was to Scott that the dying Nelson addressed his last words.

**Cawthorn Roman Camps**                          C2
*Ryedale. Ancient site off A170, 4m NW of Pickering*
This group of four Roman camps lies at the edge of Cropton Forest, and is a short distance on foot from the minor road running E from *Cawthorne*, N of the A170, to *Newton-on-Rawcliffe*. The site is tree-lined on three sides, and has a magnificent view across the moors on the fourth. All that remain are the huge embankments that formed the site boundaries of the camps on the S side of the moors.

From here a Roman road crosses *Wheeldale Moor* (near *\*Goathland*) to a camp at *Lease Rigg* near Grosmont in Esk Dale. This is thought to have been part of a longer route linking the garrison town Malton (at the SW edge of the Vale of Pickering) with the late Roman coastal forts. **Wade's Causeway**, as it is called, is considered one of Britain's best-preserved stretches of Roman road, especially in its middle section; easiest access is from Egton Bridge or Grosmont across the moor to Pickering. This minor road is extremely narrow, and unsurfaced in the part passing through Cropton Forest where it crosses the causeway at a ford.

**Clapham** see *Ingleton*

**Cleveland Hills**                               C1/C2
*N Yorks. Between North York Moors National Park & Plain of York*
This high, wild and sparsely-populated tableland, forming part of the North Yorkshire Moors National Park, reaches a height of 1490ft at Botton Head on *Urra Moor* at the head of Bilsdale. The range stretches

*North Yorkshire Moors Railway, Goathland Station*

*Newby Hall  Opposite: Hubberholme in Wharfedale*

SW in a shallow S-shaped arc from E of
*Guisborough* in the N to the neighbourhood
of Osmotherley in the S, where it merges into
the Hambleton Hills.

The steep W and N flanks drop to the Vale
of Mowbray and the valley of the Tees; from
these plains the distinctive heights of *Hasty
Bank*, *Cold Moor*, *Cringle Moor* and *Carlton
Bank* mark the progress of the *Cleveland
Way* and the *Lyke Wake Walk*, which follow
ancient monks' and miners' tracks across the
moors. They pass through part of the
**Cleveland Forest** on the escarpment
overlooking Teesside, where *Clay Bank* is a
noted viewpoint, with Forestry Commission
picnic places and trails. (See also *North
Yorkshire Forests*.) On the hills' far N flank
above the village of *Great Ayton*, Easby
Moor has a *monument* to Captain Cook; a little
further N can be seen the sandstone pinnacle
of *Roseberry Topping*, a prominent landmark.

On the S, the hills are riven with beautiful
dales running S to the Vale of Pickering. On
*Westerdale Moor* near the head of Farndale
the River Esk rises and flows N to Esk Dale,
then E to Whitby and the North Sea.

As these bleak moorland hills are largely
bracken and heather-clad, the chief
occupation here is sheep farming; iron ore
was mined until the last century.

## Cleveland Way C1/C2
*N Yorks. Long-distance footpath partly in North York
Moors National Park*

The Cleveland Way was opened in 1969, and
is 93m long. The route commences (or ends)
in *Helmsley* market place and generally
follows the W, N and E boundaries of the
*North Yorkshire Moors* which account for
about 75% of the total distance.

From Helmsley, at the edge of the Vale of
Pickering, the route passes near *Rievaulx
Abbey* and *Terrace* and arrives at *Sutton
Bank*, where a 2m deviation can be made to
Roulston Scar and the *Kilburn White Horse*;
from these points there are magnificent views
across the Plain of York. The Way continues
N on the *Hambleton Drove Road* and along
the top of the steep-sided *Hambleton Hills*,
past *Gormire Lake* and *Whitestone Cliff* to
*Osmotherley*; from here it skirts the high,
wild moors of the *Cleveland Hills*, following
the *Lyke Wake Walk* as far as Cockayne
Head above Bransdale, where it turns N and
the Walk continues E. This stretch also
follows the boundaries of the Cleveland
Forest, which is managed by the Forestry
Commission.

At *Guisborough* the route turns E for the
North Sea; just S of Guisborough, above
Great Ayton, a deviation arrives at Easby

Moor and Captain Cook's *monument*; further
N is the conspicuous sandstone outcrop of
*Roseberry Topping* (see *Great Ayton*).

From Saltburn on the coast there follows a
45m stretch along towering cliffs through
*Staithes*, *Runswick Bay*, *Sandsend*,
*Whitby*, *Robin Hood's Bay*, and
*Scarborough* to journey's end at Filey Brigg
(just N of *Filey*).

## Coverdale B2
*N Yorks. Minor dale connecting Wensleydale & A684
with Wharfedale & B6160*

The little River Cover joins the Ure between
Middleham and East Witton, after tumbling
down the dale from its source on the slopes of
Great Whernside (SE) which overlooks
Wharfedale. Not far from the rivers'
confluence (2m W) the Cover passes under a
delightful hump-backed bridge close to the
remains of 15th-c. *Coverham Abbey*, a
Premonstratensian foundation (see *East
Witton*). The bridge is the focus of a network
of little roads that come into the lower dale
from various parts of Wensleydale; this lower
part of the dale is given to racing stables and
horse-rearing, and near the village of *Carlton*
on the W bank of the Cover beneath *Penhill* is
a large cheese factory. On the E side of the
river is *Caldbergh Hall*, the birthplace of the
biblical scholar Miles Coverdale (see *East
Witton*).

Beyond Carlton the route follows the river
SW, skirting the flanks of Little and Great
Whernside before dropping down to
*Kettlewell* via *Park Rash*. This ancient
drovers' route, a gated road restricted to
lighter vehicles, passes through wild, lonely
and rugged landscape with breathtaking
views.

## Coverham Abbey see *East Witton*

## Coxwold C2
*N Yorks. Village off A19, 6m N of Easingwold*

Coxwold is situated on a gently sloping
hillside on the SW edge of the Hambleton
Hills, its main street bordered by old stone
houses and cottages, 17th-c. almshouses and
the *Old Hall* with wide grass verges in front.
Near the top of the street stands the
handsome Perpendicular **St Michael's
Church**, noted for its octagonal tower. Its
interior has a fine three-decker pulpit and
altar rails, medieval stained glass and old
monuments, including one by Grinling
Gibbons to the Earl of Fauconberg. In the
churchyard lies the Rev Laurence Sterne
who was the incumbent for the last eight
years of his life (1760-68). His home was
almost opposite the church at **Shandy Hall**,

the medieval house (later altered and added to) where he wrote *The Sentimental Journey* and *Journal to Eliza*, and completed *Tristram Shandy*. The house contains a considerable collection of books, pictures and memorabilia connected with the author.

*The Fauconberg Arms*, a hostelry of some repute, is named after the Earl who married Mary, daughter of Oliver Cromwell. Their home, **Newburgh Priory**, stands in parkland with a lake and pleasant gardens to the S of the village. The priory was an Augustinian establishment founded in 1145, but after the Dissolution it was converted into a fine mansion which now shows mainly 18th-c. work. There is a tradition that Cromwell's body is interred in a tomb which has never been opened, but which is on view in the house. Mary Fauconberg is supposed to have had secret information that the restoration of the monarchy was imminent and, being apprehensive of possible Royalist vengeance, arranged for her father's body to be removed from Westminster Abbey to the priory. The house contains many family portraits, and some fine furniture.

**Craven** A2
*N Yorks. Yorkshire Dales National Park*
The Craven hills in Yorkshire's W dales include the sources of the Rivers Ribble, Aire and Wharfe, and the smooth, familiar outlines of the 'three peaks' of *Whernside*, *Ingleborough* and *Pen-y-Ghent*, long limestone hills riddled with pot-holes and topped with millstone grit.

The striking features of the limestone landscape here include *Malham Cove* near the village of *\*Malham* and the impressive *Giggleswick Scar* between *\*Ingleton* and *\*Settle*, both results of the complex series of Craven Faults by which the Aire Gap near *\*Skipton* divides the Southern from the Central Pennines. The Craven district, well-known to the Brigantes and the Romans who mined the hills, provides valuable study for geologists, botanists and archaeologists, and recreation for hikers, climbers, cavers and sightseers. (See also *\*Pennine Way*.)

**Dalesway** A2/A3/B3
*Wharfedale. Long-distance footpath*
Linking with the *\*Ebor Way* at *\*Ilkley*, the 73m Dalesway commences at Ilkley *Old Bridge*, follows the River Wharfe and enters the *\*Yorkshire Dales National Park* at *\*Bolton Abbey*. It continues to the dale head, passes *\*Hubberholme* and follows W along *Langstrothdale*, then takes to the fells around the head of Ribblesdale and along Dentdale in Cumbria. Following the course of the

River Lune N along the far W edge of the National Park, the footpath turns W and continues to the Kent valley, terminating at Bowness-on-Windermere.

The route traverses splendid and varied scenery, passes attractive villages and approaches the glories of the Lake District. Unlike its contemporaries it is not a newly created path, but links a series of ancient tracks through its entire length. Around the head of Ribblesdale on *Cam Fell*, it meets the *\*Pennine Way*.

**Dalby Forest** see *Thornton Dale*

**Danby** C2
*Esk Dale. Village off A171, 13m W of Whitby. Nat Park Inf: (0287) 60654*
Danby stands surrounded by open moorland on the N bank of the salmon-rich Esk. *Danby Beacon*, rising 988ft NE of the village, has panoramic views of coast, dale and moor.

At *Danby Lodge* (½m E) the National Park **Moors Centre** has lectures, film shows and displays which illustrate moorland life, geology and natural history. In the extensive grounds are nature trails and picnic places; refreshments are available at the Lodge.

Opposite the Lodge and S of the river is the 14th-c. *Danby Castle*, partly ruined and now incorporated into a farmhouse. Still remaining are a spiral staircase, vaulted dungeon, two massive towers and some walls with fireplace and window apertures. Catherine Parr, sixth and last wife of Henry VIII, lived here when she was married to her second (and previous) husband Lord Latimer. The castle was approached by a packhorse bridge (*Duck Bridge*), which now makes a delightful picnic place.

3m S of Danby at the head of Danby Dale is *Botton* village, a community of handicapped people and their helpers run by the Camphill Village Trust. Visitors are welcome to the craft workshops, and there is a gift shop and coffee bar.

**Danes' Dyke** see *Flamborough Head*

**Denton Hall** see *Ilkley*

**Easby Abbey** B2
*N Yorks. Off B6271, 1m E of Richmond*
The ruins of the Premonstratensian abbey, and the parish church within its precinct, are delightfully situated on a bank of the River Swale at the end of a narrow lane. The abbey was founded in 1155 by Roald, Constable of Richmond Castle, and it flourished until the Dissolution.

Apart from the 14th-c. *N chapel*, the abbey church which stood at the centre of the complex has virtually disappeared, but other substantial remains include the *Infirmary* wing and *Abbot's Lodging* N of the church, and S, the shell of the *Refectory* with its fine windows. Set apart from the abbey is the handsome early 14th-c. *Gatehouse* with an upper room where the abbot held court, which is reached by an external staircase.

**St Agatha's Church**, founded in 1148, possesses some remarkable 13th-c. frescoes whose quality is surpassed in Yorkshire only by those at the Church of St Peter and St Paul in *\*Pickering*. The paintings include biblical and rural scenes. Another treasure is a *replica* of the Easby Cross, the original of which is in London's Victoria and Albert Museum. The carving on its face shows Christ in Majesty with the Disciples, while the back has animals and birds among foliage and fruit. The church has an early Norman font and the glass in the E window is six centuries old. Over the arched ceiling of the porch is a priest's room.

The wooded hamlet and its Georgian *Hall* stand above the abbey and church, which can be reached from Richmond by taking the footpath along the river. In St Mary's Parish Church at *\*Richmond* can be seen some early 16th-c. canopied stalls, taken from Easby when it was dissolved. W of Richmond are the fells and moors of Swaledale.

**East Witton**                                B2
*Wensleydale. Village off A6108, 4m SE of Leyburn*
The main road skirts the E end of the village which remains a most pleasant backwater, the old stone cottages and houses ranged along both sides of a long, wide, tree-clad green nestling below Witton Fell. The *Church of St John the Evangelist* stands on the main road a little apart from the village. Both were built by the Earl of Aylesbury: the church between 1809 and 1812 to commemorate the Golden Jubilee of George III, and the village, which replaced an earlier settlement, to serve the Jervaulx Abbey estate.

A small road leads W beneath *Braithwaite Moor*, with its relics of coal and iron mining, to *\*Coverdale*; the road passes a 17th-c. farmhouse, *Braithwaite Hall* (NT), which may be visited by arrangement with the tenant. Standing in 748 acres of farm and moorland, the Hall's architecture is characteristic of its date (1667). The road arrives at Coverham, where a charming hump-backed *bridge* crosses the Cover. Near here on private land are the insubstantial

remains of *Coverham Abbey*, a
Premonstratensian foundation. The
*Gatehouse* is really all that is left: a large part
of the main buildings have been used as
building material for a private residence on
the site, although bits and pieces are
scattered about the gardens. The old *Abbey
Mill* and the 18th-c. *Miller's House* nearby
have been substantially restored, and fit in
with their idyllic surroundings.

Another interesting farmhouse, *Caldbergh
Hall*, is to be seen just up-river. This is the
birthplace of Miles Coverdale the biblical
scholar, who translated the Bible and
Apocrypha from German and Latin versions;
his work was first published in 1535. The
*Book of Common Prayer* retains the Psalms of
this translation, and the Authorised Version
of the Bible of 1611 owes much to this man
from one of the most remote parts of
Yorkshire.

## Ebor Way                                    C2/C3
*N & W Yorks. Long-distance footpath*

The Ebor Way takes its name from
*Eboracum*, the Roman name for York; it is
70m long and was opened in 1983. Joining
the *Cleveland Way* at Helmsley with the
*Dalesway* at Ilkley, the route passes through
*York*, Tadcaster and Wetherby. Its opening
allows ramblers to cover 316m along
designated footpaths from Windermere in
Cumbria to the Humber via the Cleveland
and Wolds Ways.

## Egton Bridge                                  C2
*Esk Dale. Village off A171, 8m SW of Whitby. Event:
Gooseberry Show (1st Tue in Aug)*

This pretty village lies deep in a wooded
valley on the banks of the Esk. The river here
is picturesque, with an island reached by
stepping stones near a weir, and a colony of
water fowl.

**St Hedda's Roman Catholic Church**
(1866) has a plain appearance from the
outside, but the interior is ornate with carved
and decorated tableaux of the Stations of the
Cross, some fine statuary, a beautiful reredos
and a frescoed ceiling in the chancel
illustrating events in the life of Christ. This
was the parish of Father Nicholas Postgate,
martyred for his faith at York at the age of 83
in 1679. On the N exterior wall are more
tableaux of the Stations of the Cross and
behind the church a grotto of the Virgin. At
the annual Gooseberry Show here,
competitors are said to produce fruit the size
of hens' eggs.

**Ellerton Priory** see *Reeth*

## Esk Dale                                      C1/C2
*N Yorks. Dale S of A171 in North York Moors
National Park*

The Esk, a fine salmon river, rises on
Westerdale Moor in the Cleveland Hills and
flows eastward 24m to the sea at Whitby. Esk
Dale contains some of the Park's finest
scenery: wild and open moorland in the
upper reaches, rolling expanses of
pastureland as the valley broadens, and
thickly wooded slopes in the lower reaches.

Unclassified roads wind from side to side
of this deep valley, which has some of the
steepest hills in the country. The S side is
joined by several short dales cutting deeply
through the high moorland – *Westerdale*,
*Danby Dale*, *Little* and *Great Fryup Dales*,
*Glaisdale* and the valley of the *Murk Esk*. The
distinctive high ridge-lands between these
close-set dales are called 'riggs'.

The only town in Esk Dale is *Whitby* at
the mouth of the estuary, but there are
several scattered villages including
*Castleton*; *Danby* with its National Park
Moors Centre; *Lealholm* with a quoits pitch
on the green; *Glaisdale* with a packhorse
*bridge* dated 1619; *Egton Bridge*; *Grosmont*,
at the N end of the popular *North Yorkshire
Moors Railway*. Boating is available along the
river between *Sleights* and *Ruswarp*, which
have delightful riverside cafés.

British Rail's Middlesbrough-Whitby line
has a section following the river through Esk
Dale; known as the *Esk Valley Line*, it stops
at many attractive places along its route.

## Farndale                                      C2
*Ryedale. Dale off A170, N of Kirkbymoorside*

This lovely deep valley cutting S for 7m from
the North Yorkshire Moors has the pretty
River Dove flowing through on its way to join
the Rye in the Vale of Pickering. There are
three small communities, *Church Houses* (N),
*Low Mill* and *Lownd* (S). A little way below
Lownd, the road running N from the A170 at
*Kirkbymoorside* ascends *Pan Nab* by
*Gillamoor Church*; a 'surprise view' gives a
wonderful panorama E over Farndale to
Blakey Ridge and Spaunton Moor beyond.

The dale is especially beautiful in spring,
when its renowned display of wild daffodils
covers the river banks. At this time volunteer
wardens patrol Farndale, a locally-designated
*Nature Reserve*, to protect the blooms. Little
can be seen from the roads, however, and it is
advisable to leave cars in the park at *Low Mill*
and take the signposted path up the dale
beside the Dove; this way the daffodils can be
seen in all their glory. Although the walk is
fine at any time of year, spring with its
daffodils makes it a special experience.

## Filey
D2

*N Yorks. Town on A1039 (A165), 8m SE of Scarborough. Event: Edwardian Festival (1st week in Jul). EC Wed. Inf: Tel (0723) 512204/372261*

This quiet and select little resort at the N end of Filey Bay is sheltered by the wedge-shaped headland called *Car Naze*, formerly a Roman signal station terminating in the natural breakwater of *Filey Brigg*. Both Naze and Brigg are within easy walking distance of the town and ideal for bird watching in spring and autumn; the Brigg is also good for angling. Projecting far into the sea, the Brigg is under water at high tide, and in heavy seas the sight of foam and waves is quite spectacular.

*Filey beach* is the best on the Yorkshire coast, and extends along the bay; the 4m sands are firm and dry, and there is safe bathing. The bay is popular with yachtsmen and wind-surfers. Seaside amusements are to be found near the slipway at *Coble Landing*, where the few cobles and the lifeboat are brought to the water by tractor. From here the promenade extends to the S end of the town, where a steep hill leads up to the hotels and shops. Here also are the *Seafront Gardens, Sun Lounge, Theatre* and *Concert Hall*. In Queen Street, **Filey Folk Museum** has lifeboat memorabilia among displays from Victorian times and the 17th c.

Filey Brigg marks the termination of the *\*Cleveland Way* and the start of the *\*Wolds Way*, which continues the long-distance walk inland; the coastal walk SE from here follows magnificent fossil-rich cliffs to *\*Bempton Cliffs* with its bird reserve, and *\*Flamborough Head*.

## Flamborough Head
D3

*Humberside. Off B1255, 6m NE of Bridlington*

This striking chalk headland marks the NE point of the *\*Yorkshire Wolds*; its heavily indented coastline is riddled with caves and stacks, and the headland has natural harbours, *North* and *South Landings*, situated in clefts of the cliffs to either side. The village of *Flamborough* (2m inland) stands on the road connecting South Landing with its counterpart, where there is a lifeboat station; the village *Church* is dedicated to St Oswald, patron saint of seamen.

The area is good for bird watching in spring and autumn, and the spectacular 11m cliff walk NW past the *\*Bempton Cliffs* bird reserve to the resort of *\*Filey*, and Filey Brigg, also attracts fossil collectors. Visitors flock in summer to the old fishing town and modern resort of *\*Bridlington* occupying the sheltered corner on Bridlington Bay to the SW of the headland.

Just E of Sewerby at Bridlington, across the neck of the headland, is a defensive ditch called **Danes' Dyke**; as much as 20ft deep and 60ft wide in parts, this 2½m entrenchment is thought to pre-date the Bronze Age and to have been used by the Brigantian tribe. A *Nature Trail* can be followed along its length. In 1779, two British men-of-war were captured off the headland after a battle with a French squadron displaying American colours, commanded by the renegade Scot John Paul Jones who, with the French, fought on the American side in the War of Independence. More ships have been claimed by the sea than by battles, and the tip of the headland is surmounted by a *Lighthouse* and *Fog-signal Station*; the lighthouse was built in 1806 to replace *Beacon Tower*, an octagonal stone edifice standing a little way inland; it was from this 17th-c. tower with its flaming beacon that the headland got its name. The Head has a holiday camp, caravan site, golf course and farms.

**Forge Valley** see *Hackness*

## Fountains Abbey and Studley Royal Park (NT)
B3

*N Yorks. Off B6265 (Studley Royal), 3m SW of Ripon*

Set in a narrow valley, through which the River Skell flows to join the Ure at Ripon, the massive ruined Cistercian Abbey of Fountains is one of England's great ecclesiastical monuments. In 1132 the site was granted to dissident Benedictine monks from St Mary's Abbey, York, who desired to live a stricter disciplinary life as Cistercians. The monastery that they built, however, grew in power and by the time of the Dissolution was very wealthy.

Sold by Henry VIII to Sir Richard Gresham, the abbey was ultimately used as a source of building stone for the nearby Fountains Hall. It was saved from further destruction only by the care of William Aislabie when it became part of his Studley Royal estate in 1768. William extended the **Studley Royal Park**, his father John Aislabie's creation of formal parkland graced with riverside lawns, lakes, temples and classical statuary, providing a beautiful setting for England's best preserved and most magnificent abbey ruin.

The full splendour of the ruin is best appreciated from the *Gatehouse*, with the abbey church's 168ft tower on the left, then the well-preserved W front and the long range of the cellarium extending over the Skell, the whole set in spacious and beautifully kept lawns. The Perpendicular tower is Tudor, but the rest of the Abbey dates from the 12th-13th c. Outstanding features of the *Church* are the *nave*, with 11 bays still intact, and the *Chapel of the Nine Altars* at the E end, dominated by a 60ft-high window which complements a similar window over the W doorway, 370ft away. Of the other abbey buildings grouped around the cloister, the most remarkable is the *cellarium* on the W side. 300ft long, it has a central line of 19 piers supporting a low vault on either side.

During the early autumn the Abbey is floodlit, and made more beautiful by the sound of chanting monks heard from the precincts – an entirely modern *Son et Lumiere*, since the plainsong is relayed by tape.

Between the ancient bridge and the gatehouse is the *Abbey Mill* and *Fountains Hall*, a fine example of early 17th-c. domestic architecture. The classical symmetry of the façade, with two ranges flanking a recessed doorway, is complemented by gables, a battlemented skyline and many mullioned and transomed windows. Crowning the central door with its Ionic columns is a balustraded balcony enriched by stone knights in armour overlooked by a fine tall, narrow bay window. Inside, there is a central hall and minstrels' gallery, an enormous fireplace with a sculptured panel depicting the Judgement of Solomon, and a window with 60 shields. One of the items on display is the foundation charter of Fountains Abbey, another is a model showing it as it was at the Dissolution. The Hall has been temporarily closed to the public for use as the headquarters of the Fountains Abbey Appeal.

To the N of the abbey complex is **Studley Royal Park**, a huge well-planned parkland with delightful walks up and down the valley sides, through woodland and across open spaces of lawns and flower-beds, past temples and statues and beside lakes formed by the canalization of the banks of the Skell. The *Deer Park*, with its acres of rolling meadowland and magnificent trees supports herds of Red, Fallow and Sika deer and includes a lake with a collection of waterfowl. The parkland was laid out in the 18th c. by John Aislabie, when he was Chancellor of the Exchequer, as part of the Studley Hall Estate. After being destroyed by fire in 1946 the Hall has been rebuilt, but is not open to the public. The E end of the park can be approached from the village of *Studley Roger*, and has a large parking area with a beautiful lake view.

The village **Church of St Mary the Virgin** stands just inside the park. It was built in 1871 by William Burges for the Marchioness of Ripon to commemorate her brother, F. Grantham Vyner, who had been murdered by Greek brigands. The spire is 152ft high and the exterior has many fine details, the W doorway with 21 birds in its quatrefoils, the porch with sculptures of the Virgin, an angel and a dove.

The interior is remarkable for its marble embellishments: the font of Tennessee marble with representations of infancy, youth, manhood and old age; the credance table of Californian marble; the columns of Purbeck marble, and the chancel steps of Sicilian marble and Belgian porphyry representing man's fall, redemption and purification; and the Egyptian alabaster chancel walls with marble mosaic borders and paving in which are shown some of Jerusalem's principal buildings. A screen of alabaster and marble encloses a chapel with the marble tomb of the 1st Marquis and Marchioness of Ripon.

**Fountains Hall** see *Fountains Abbey*

**Fylingdales Early Warning Station** see *Goathland*

**Ganton** see *Scarborough*

**Gillamoor** see *Farndale*

**Gilling East**                                    C2
*Ryedale. Village on B1363, 4m S of Helmsley*

Gilling East stands in the valley of the Holbeck between the Hambleton and the Howardian Hills. Many of the village's stone cottages and houses are approached by wooden bridges over a tributary of the beck which flows alongside the main street. High above, almost lost in thick overhanging woodland, is the 14th-c. **Castle** acquired in 1930 by *Ampleforth College* for its junior school.

The castle, which shows an intriguing mixture of styles, originated as a 14th-c. tower-house over which stands a block that is partly Elizabethan and partly early 18th-c. The flanking wings are also early 18th-c. The interiors are rich in plasterwork and wood carving. The unique glass and panelling of the *Great Chamber* (which dates from 1585) were sold to Randolph Hearst the American millionaire in 1929, but restored to Gilling in 1952. The Long Gallery still resides in the Bowes Museum at Barnard Castle in County Durham.

The clock of the *Church of the Holy Cross* was given by the great Indian cricketer, Prince Ranjitsinhji, who lived for a time at the rectory.

## Goathland C2
*N Yorks. Village off A169, 9m SW of Whitby. EC Wed, Sat*

Isolated in a sea of moorland, Goathland is one of the most delightful villages in the North York Moors National Park. Cottages, houses, hotels and shops, and the pleasant late Victorian Church, *St Mary's*, are widely scattered along broad verges cropped by free-ranging sheep.

The village is situated on the route of the *North Yorkshire Moors Railway* which has a station here, the penultimate halt on the picturesque 18m journey between Grosmont and Pickering. There is a 3½m Historical Railway Trail to Grosmont which follows the original track of the Pickering-Whitby line, including the former rope-worked incline. The Eller Beck, which rises on the SE moors, meets the railway about 2m S of the station, where the A169 crosses the beck. Nearby is the *Fylingdales Early Warning Station*, which lies by the route of the *Lyke Wake Walk* on its last stretch to the coast and to *Fen Bog*, a 40-acre nature reserve managed by the Yorkshire Wildlife Trust.

This striking, if sombre, complex is one of three in the Western world and is notable for its three large white 'golf ball' radomes which are visible for miles around. Each radome encloses a radar and computerised communications system capable of giving four minutes' warning of a nuclear attack – and of detecting an object as small as a tea-tray over Moscow.

A small detour made from the area of the Early Warning Station leads to an ancient wayfarers' cross on **Lilla Howe**, reputedly the grave of Lilla who gave his life for his master, King Edwin of Northumbria, in 626AD.

Just W of Goathland on West Beck, which runs S to join Eller Beck, is the noted beauty spot, **Mallyan Spout**. A track leads upstream to another waterfall, *Nelly Ayre Foss*; close by a well preserved stretch of the Roman road from *Cawthorn Roman Camps* can be reached.

N of Goathland are two beautiful hamlets, Beck Hole and Darnholme, from which the waterfalls *Thomason Foss* and *Water Ark Force* are easily accessible. Both hamlets are on Eller Beck, the road to *Darnholme* terminating where the beck is crossed by a ford and stepping stones. *Beck Hole*'s few

cottages, and *Birch Hall Inn*, cluster round a tiny green on which quoits is played; the hamlet stands at the bottom of 1-in-4 hills where Eller Beck joins the Murk Esk to flow N through the Esk Valley to Grosmont.

## Gouthwaite Reservoir see *Ramsgill*

## Grassington A3
*Wharfedale. Village on B6265, 9m N of Skipton. EC Thur. Nat Park Inf: Tel (0756) 752748*

Now one of the least attractive of the upper dales villages, with much commercial and residential development having taken place this century. The delightful cobbled *Market Square* with its attendant alleys survives as the tourist attraction, together with the riverside down the hill near the early 17th-c. *bridge*. The old cottages and attractive cafés, inns and shops make this village something of a metropolis between the river's source and Ilkley, and this may account for Grassington's ability to draw more visitors than any other village in the valley.

In the square, occupying two old cottages, the **Upper Wharfedale Museum** portrays past life in the upper dale; displays include farming and rural items, and collections of veterinary instruments, flints and minerals. The National Park Centre is at Colvend (see *Further Information*, p. 25).

Grassington was the lead mining centre of Wharfedale, and the old workings are still to be seen scattered over the moors. The mines' heyday came in the 18th and 19th c; by the end of the 19th c. they were worked out, and also suffered from the opening up of overseas mines. The Romans mined for lead, and before them the Brigantes: the moorlands stretching from here W to Malham and E to Pateley Bridge, now the domain of potholers and caving enthusiasts, are rich in prehistoric remains. The popular *Stump Cross Caverns* are off the Pateley Bridge road.

1m NW of the village a minor road following the Wharfe on its E bank towards *Kettlewell* passes *Grass Wood*, a Nature Reserve owned by the Yorkshire Wildlife Trust. Here are many rare species of flora growing on the limestone.

## Great Ayton C1
*N Yorks. Village on A173, 3m NE of Stokesley*

This is a village of old houses clustered around greens, on the banks of the River Leven. It has the Quaker public school, the *Friends' School* (1842), facing High Green; nearby on the riverside is the *Old School*. The family of Captain Cook moved here from Marton-in-Cleveland when he was eight years old, so that his father could become bailiff to the Lord of the Manor, Mr Skottowe, at Airy Holme Farm. Skottowe paid for the lad's schooling for five years, until he left to take up an apprenticeship with a grocer in *Staithes.

The old farm is still in use, and the Old School's upper room is now a **Museum** containing mementoes of Cook's schooldays; it is reached by an external staircase. The graves of Cook's mother and five of her children are in *All Saints'* churchyard, as is that of Skottowe, who lived at *Ayton Hall* next to the church.

In 1934 the Cooks' cottage was demolished stone by stone and transferred to Fitzroy Gardens, Melbourne, Australia. On the site where it stood is an obelisk of stones brought from Cape Everard near Point Hicks, Victoria, the first point on the Australian continent sighted by Cook (April 20, 1770). Above the village near the *Cleveland Way* on *Easby Moor* is a **monument** erected in 1827 to his memory: from here and from **Roseberry Topping** (NT), a striking 1057ft pinnacle to the NE, views stretch far over the moors and to the North Sea.

Another Cook memorial is the **Captain Cook Birthplace Museum** in Stewart Park, *Marton* (now part of Middlesbrough), 8m NW. Exhibits here are devoted to Cook's life and voyages of exploration, and the natural history and ethnography of the South Seas. This is the starting point of the *Cook Trail* S to *Whitby*.

## Grinton
A2

*Swaledale. Village off B6270, 9m W of Richmond*

Stretching along Grinton Beck on the S bank of the Swale, Grinton was once the termination of the Corpse Way which started near the dale head at *Keld*. Carried on wicker biers from outlying settlements, the dead were laid to rest in the churchyard of *St Andrew's*, then known as the 'Church of Swaledale'. The medieval parish stretched the dale's length: 20m from Richmond to Keld.

On the hill S of the village is a castellated building that was once a shooting lodge, but is now a popular *Youth Hostel*. W of Grinton is **Maiden Castle**, a Romano-British entrenchment in an excellent state of preservation; there are earthworks, barrows and cairns on the fells around the village. E of Grinton, further down-river, the ruins of *Marrick Priory* and *Ellerton Priory* stand on either side of the river bank (see *Reeth*).

**Grosmont** see *North Yorkshire Moors Railway*

## Guisborough
C1

*Cleveland. Pop 14,860. 8m NE of Stokesley (A171/A173). EC Wed MD Thur, Sat*

Formerly in Yorkshire's North Riding, this busy market town lies at the base of the *Cleveland Hills* where the N escarpment drops to the coastal plain. It has a tree-lined, cobble-edged main street with a medley of old red-roofed buildings and an ancient cross with sundial and ball in the market place. It grew around its Augustinian Priory, St Mary.

Surrounded by trees, the gaunt remains of the **Priory** rise near the 15th-c. parish *Church of St Nicholas*. Founded in 1119 by Robert de Bruis, this once-wealthy priory is reduced to little more than its *Gatehouse, c. 1200*, and its lofty 13th-c. E end with a great 24ft wide x 60ft high window flanked by the windows of the *choir aisles*. De Bruis' fine 16th-c. *cenotaph*, formerly in the priory, can be seen in the church. The *Cleveland Way*, which has an extension to Captain Cook's Monument above *Great Ayton* and to nearby *Roseberry Topping*, passes near Guisborough on its route to the sea at *Saltburn*.

## Hackness
D2

*N Yorks. Village off A171, 6m NW of Scarborough*

This pretty village nestles in a wooded valley on Lowdales Beck in the *Tabular Hills*, the shelf-like plateau running W-E between the Vale of Pickering and the North Yorkshire Moors. The *Hall* with its fine pedimented portico dates from 1791 and has pleasant gardens, fine parkland and a lake. It is the seat of Lord Derwent.

**St Peter's Church** occupies the site of an Anglo-Saxon nunnery (7th-9th-c.); the chancel arch is thought to date at least from the 11th c., some say earlier, and there are the remains of an early Anglo-Saxon cross with an Ogham inscription. Other inscriptions on the cross fragments bear the name Abbadissa Oedilburga. The nunnery had close connections with Whitby Abbey in the 8th c.

Hackness is situated N of the beautiful *Forge Valley*, where the River Derwent flows S from Fylingdales Moor.

The Nature Conservancy Council's *Forge Valley Nature Reserve* has woodland trails and a car park which occupies the site of an iron works originating from the 13th c., and which gave the valley its name. The reserve's native woodlands shelter many plants and birds. Beyond Hackness, a steep and winding road with fine views leads N to the locality of *Silpho* in Wykeham Forest, where the Forestry Commission has a 2-3m waymarked *Walk*. This shows good examples of fossils and plants found in the

Corallian rock of the Tabular Hills. Further along the road, *Reasty* car park has fine views over moor, forest and farm, and from here the Forestry Commission waymarked *Trail* (16m) leads through Wykeham and Dalby Forests to *Allerston*. (See also *Thornton Dale*, *North Yorkshire Forests* and *Walk 5*, p. 23.)

## Hambleton Hills                                    B2/C2
*N Yorks. W of Vale of Pickering*

This steep-sided range embracing the SW corner of the North York Moors National Park reaches a height of 1257ft and extends about 20m from Osmotherley in the N to Ampleforth in the S. Here the Holbeck flows E through the Gilling Gap to meet the River Rye, thus separating the Hambletons from the Howardian Hills which range SE to form the SW corner of the Vale of Pickering.

Clothed with woodland or heather and punctuated by steep ravines, the range forms upper Ryedale's W flank and declines sharply W along the Vale of Mowbray, fertile land to the N of Thirsk and Northallerton. The escarpment has far-reaching views over the plain, notably from the famed *Sutton Bank*; just S is the *White Horse* of *Kilburn*, which can be seen from far across the plain.

A spur of the long-distance walk, the *Cleveland Way*, follows a Forestry Commission walk (Hambleton Forest) from Sutton Bank to the White Horse.

## Hampsthwaite                                    B3
*Nidderdale. Village off A59/A61/B6451, 3m NW of Harrogate*

Hampsthwaite stands at a point where the Roman road between Aldborough and Ilkley forded the River Nidd. Now the Nidd is crossed by a narrow stone-buttressed bridge on the N side of this delightful village, probably the most attractive in the dale. The **Church of St Thomas à Becket** stands near the green, and there is a well preserved packhorse bridge behind the village hall.

For many generations this was the home of the Thackeray family, some of whom rest in the churchyard; William Makepeace Thackeray is said to have stayed here occasionally. Amy Woodforde-Finden (d. 1919), composer of the 'Indian Love Lyrics', has a white marble cenotaph in the church; she lies recumbent, crowned with laurel and guarded by cherubs; round the base some of her well-known songs are depicted in a beautiful and realistic manner. Her grave is in the churchyard.

**Hardrow Force** see *Hawes*

## Harewood House                                    B3
*Wharfedale. Historic house on A61 (A659), 7m S of Harrogate*

The estate village dates mainly from the 18th c. There are still many attractive houses of the period, although there has been some modern development. The interesting *Castle* ruins stand apart from the village, where the road takes a sharp curve on Harewood Bank, and can be seen effectively when the trees are without leaves. Of Norman foundation and reconstructed in the mid-14th c., the castle can be visited with permission from the Estate Office.

Harewood House was built for the Lascelles family between 1759 and 1767 by the eminent York architect John Carr, who also designed the village; the family has lived here ever since. The present occupant is the 7th Earl of Harewood, elder son of the late Princess Royal and cousin of Queen Elizabeth II.

Built of stone from the estate, the house's classical N façade by Carr contrasts with Sir Charles Barry's rebuilding of the S front in the early Victorian style (1843). A further contrast is between Barry's terraces and formal garden and the landscaping of the parkland (by 'Capability' Brown, 1772).

Harewood's exquisite interiors were designed by Robert Adam and are characteristic of his early work. Also typical of Adam is his collaboration with master craftsworkers of the period, exemplified by the stucco work of Joseph Rose in the *Entrance Hall*, or wall and ceiling panels in the *Music Room* by Antonio Zucchi and by his wife Angelica Kauffmann, all to Adam designs.

On view are superb items of furniture made specially for the house by Thomas Chippendale, fine collections of Chinese and Sèvres porcelain and Leeds Ware, and a magnificent collection of paintings by English and Italian masters.

The *Grounds* still reflect the work of 'Capability' Brown, despite a severe storm in 1967 which damaged numerous trees. A modern attraction is the *Harewood Bird Garden* with a Tropical House holding a marvellous collection of humming birds, while the Tropical Area below exhibits fauna and flora typical of desert, rain forest and riverside. There is a penguin pool, as well as a lake with flamingos and various water fowl. An adventure playground, picnic area, cafeteria and Courtyard Restaurant add to the attractions.

Standing apart from the house and shaded by trees is the 15th-c. church, considerably restored in the 18th and 19th c. **All Saints'** has some fine monuments, including a set of medieval alabaster figures of six recumbent couples on tomb chests: the latest and perhaps the finest shows Sir Richard Redmayne (d. 1476) with his feet resting against a lion. The communion rails were erected in memory of **George V** by his daughter, the late Princess Royal.

### Harrogate                                    B3
*N Yorks. Pop 64,620. 11m S of Ripon (A61/A6161). Events: International Youth Music Festival (Easter); Model Railway Exhibition (Easter); Flower Show (2nd week in Apr); Arts & Crafts Market (May); International Festival of Cycling (Jun); Hallé Orchestra Festival (3rd week in Jun); Cricket Festival (Jun); Great Yorkshire Show (2nd week in Jul); International Festival of Music (1st & 2nd weeks in Aug); Flower Show (2nd week in Sep); Northern Antique Dealers' Fair (3rd/4th week in Sep). EC Wed MD Mon-Sat. Inf: Tel (0423) 65912/68051*

Harrogate is conveniently situated halfway between London and Edinburgh, and between the E and W coasts. Now one of England's leading holiday resorts and a major conference, exhibition and show centre, the town began as a famous and fashionable spa where the gentry came to 'take the waters', following Sir William Slingsby's discovery of the town's first medicinal spring, the Tewit Well (1571). Subsequent discoveries revealed over 80 springs, almost half of them in the area once known as Bogs Fields and now the **Valley Gardens**.

Principal outdoor attractions centre on the 120-acre gardens, which are situated on the W side of town. The area includes woodland, shrubberies, flower beds and lawns, and has a stream running through; the 600ft glass-covered Sun Colonnade leads to the *Sun Pavilion* with its glass-domed roof, where popular band concerts are presented.

2m W of the town at **Harlow Car Gardens** are the Northern Horticultural Society's trial grounds, where rewarding hours can be spent exploring the magnificent displays of many types of gardens. *The Stray*, 200-acre horseshoe-shaped enclave on the S, forms a wide green belt around much of the town centre and is strikingly beautiful in spring, when its tree-lined verges bloom with thousands of crocuses.

Nearby is the **Royal Pump Room**, where it is still possible to 'take the waters'. The octagonal building was constructed in 1842 on the site of a sulphur well discovered in 1626; from there the water was pumped to the Royal Baths where the visitor could be immersed in foul-smelling liquid – probably only slightly less objectionable than drinking it. The Pump Room now houses a **Museum** of local history.

To the NE, overlooking Crescent Gardens, is the **Royal Baths** and **Assembly Rooms**, where Turkish Baths can be enjoyed in a Victorian atmosphere; the town's Information Centre is here. Further NE the **Conference Centre**, with seating for 2000, is the venue for large gatherings; there is also a banqueting hall seating 1000. The Centre is connected by six linked exhibition halls to the **Royal Hall**, a fine relic of the town's opulent past, capable of seating about 1300; this is used for smaller conferences, exhibitions and lectures. Concerts are also performed in both centres.

In the centre of town the *Opera House* is now used as a repertory theatre. The **Art Gallery** (1904) in Victoria Avenue, S, has a permanent collection of Victorian and 20th-c. art.

Harrogate is noted for its splendid tea rooms and locally-made toffee, and offers some of the best shopping in the provinces, particularly in antiques. The character of the town, perhaps, is best reflected in its grand hotels, dating from the early 19th c., when the town's wealth was founded.

3m SE beside the A661 are the **Plompton Rocks**, giant blocks of millstone grit standing in mixed woodland at the side of a lake. Some have been given fanciful names: 'Old Chair', 'Lovers' Leap', 'Tunnel', 'Wishing Steps'. 'Needle's Eye' has a hole through its centre. They are the product of an immense upheaval in the Carboniferous period, followed by the action of weathering and the passage of ice floes. 1½m further on lies *Spofforth Castle* (early 14th-c.), once a seat of the Percys, now ruined.

### Hawes                                      A2
*Wensleydale. Town on A684/B6255, 12m W of Aysgarth. EC Wed MD Tue. Nat Park Inf: Tel (09697) 450*

850ft above sea level, Hawes is the metropolis of the higher dale. Economically it depends on farming (particularly dairying), rope making and tourism; the narrow grey-stone streets are packed during the holiday season. The manufacture of Wensleydale cheese is not confined to Hawes, but it is despatched nationwide from here, and the town is considered to be its home.

The **Upper Dales Folk Museum** in Station Yard has displays of folk life collected by the well-known Dales' writers, Marie Hartley and Joan Ingilby. Trades and occupations of the upper dales represented include hand knitting, cheese making, farming, peat cutting and lead mining.

Encircled by lofty fells, Hawes with its *Youth Hostel* is a popular hiking centre. The

B6270 leading N to Thwaite in Swaledale crosses the well-known **Buttertubs Pass** between *Great Shunner Fell* (W) and *Lovely Seat*. The Pass rises to a height of 1726ft and gives breathtaking views, often with only the bleating of sheep and the call of curlew or grouse to break the silence of the summer months. In winter the winds howl over the tops, the mists swirl ominously and snow covers the land in ever-deepening drifts. The 'tubs' are declivities of 100ft or so, eroded in the limestone over millions of years.

The *Pennine Way* passes near **Hardrow Force** 2m N of Hawes, a spectacular waterfall reached by going through *The Green Dragon Inn* (where a small charge is made), and walking about ½m up Fossdale Gill. The water drops 100ft into a pool in a narrow ravine girt by towering cliffs. It is possible to walk along a rock ledge behind the fall, which is named after the nearby village and is the highest single-drop fall in England.

**Hayburn Wyke** (NT)                    D2
*N Yorks. Coastal feature off A171, 8m NW of Scarborough*

Woodland paths wind through 65 acres of cliffland where Hayburn Beck has carved through the boulder clay to the shore and falls to a small rocky bay. This is good fossil-hunting ground: a delightful, quiet spot which never seems to get busy, possibly because cars must be left in the *Hayburn Wyke Hotel* car park (small charge) at the top of the wooded area close to the road.

The *Cleveland Way* passes the Wyke, presenting wayfarers with a scramble down a steep path, and a footbridge across the stream (see *Walks*, p. 24). The Nature Conservancy Council manages a *Nature Reserve* here.

**Helmsley**                    C2
*Ryedale. Town on A170/B1257, 13m W of Pickering. Event: Helmsley Festival (1st week in Aug). EC Wed MD Fri. Nat Park Inf: Tel (0439) 70657. Tourist Inf: Tel (0439) 70401*

Dominated by its ruined castle, Helmsley stands on the banks of the River Rye and Borough Beck at the W end of the Vale of Pickering and at the S end of the *Cleveland Way*. It is a charming town of quaint streets and red-roofed houses built around a large, cobbled market place with a marked cross, and a canopied Gothic *monument* designed by Sir George Gilbert Scott as a memorial to the 2nd Baron Feversham.

Among the buildings around the square is the *Town Hall*, formerly the Court House, built in 1901 by the Earl of Feversham; next door the Victorian *Police Station* no longer stands for law and order, but does duty as a

café and shop. Close by is a half-timbered Elizabethan cottage, which was once the vicarage and now is incorporated with two Georgian buildings as *The Black Swan Hotel*. Behind is the 16th-c. *Canons Garth* built for the priests of Kirkham Abbey, and alongside is **All Saints' Church** N of the market place, rebuilt in Victorian Gothic but including parts of earlier buildings.

The church has some interesting wall paintings; those in the N aisle show names and shields of Archbishops of York, Abbots of Rievaulx and vicars of Helmsley set in clusters of trees and vines. In the S transept are scenes in the lives of Sts Aiden and Oswald, and a dragon being forced over a cliff by a knight. The transept is *St Columba's Chapel*, and the stained glass depicts the life of the saint. The glass in the N aisle shows incidents in the history of the town and of Rievaulx Abbey.

W of the market square, the 12th and 13th-c. **Castle** on its rocky outcrop comprises the barbican, gatehouse, domestic buildings and part of the keep. Many alterations and reconstructions have been made, but after the Civil War the castle was plundered by the townsfolk for its stone. Historically its greatest achievement was probably a three-month stand during a siege by Parliamentarians in 1644.

Off Bridge Street is **Duncombe Park**, seat of the Fevershams, a grand mansion built by Sir Charles Duncombe in 1713. The house is scheduled to be open to the public; until then, only the grounds may be visited. NW of the park is the beautiful 18th-c. landscaped *Rievaulx Terrace*, with vistas of *Rievaulx Abbey* through the trees.

Helmsley lies at the E edge of the Forestry Commission's **Hambleton Forest**, which has numerous trails, viewpoints and picnic areas.

See also *Bilsdale* and *Bransdale*.

**Herriot Country**                    A2/B2
*Swaledale & Wensleydale*

James Herriot, the Scottish-born but 'naturalised' Yorkshire vet, has brought a new popularity to the northernmost of the Yorkshire Dales. He first became known through written accounts of his experiences and those of his colleagues, bringing a breath of the Yorkshire countryside from the broad farming community they served into countless homes in Britain and overseas.

As Herriot's books were transcribed for the cinema and television, he and his environment became even more widely known. His practice was based in *Thirsk* (Darrowby), but his work took him far afield to places like *Reeth and Richmond in Swaledale, and Askrigg and Leyburn in Wensleydale; they appear in his books and films under fictitious names. Reeth and Askrigg were main filming centres, and a wild, narrow valley N of Reeth, near Langthwaite in Arkengarthdale, was the setting for the opening of each television episode.

Herriot's media work also covered other parts of Yorkshire, notably the area around *Pickering in Ryedale.

### Hole of Horcum C2
*N Yorks. Natural feature off A169, 8m NE of Pickering*

This is a huge declivity on the North Yorkshire Moors, at the head of a glen through which flows Levisham Beck. Formed by the action of glaciers and springs which have eroded the clay beneath the limestone beds, it is large enough to contain cultivable fields and is a popular hang-gliding centre. From its moorland rim on the top of *Saltersgate Bank* there are splendid views, and a car park. At the bottom of the bank is the famous *Saltersgate Inn*, so named from its position on the medieval salt traders' route between Whitby and Pickering (now the A169). From the car park here there is a 3m walk across moorland to the *Bridestones* (see also *Thornton Dale*).

### Hovingham C2
*Ryedale. Village on B1257, 8m W of Malton*

The village has been the seat of the Worsley family since 1553. The Italian-style **Hovingham Hall**, their present residence, dates from the 18th c. and is built on the site of a Roman villa, remains of which were discovered during the laying out of the gardens in 1745. Perhaps its most notable features are the arched *Gatehouse*, and a *Riding School*; the ground floor of the main building was built to house the horses, and the living rooms occupy the upper floor.

In the parkland there is a very fine *Cricket Field*, suited to a family that is associated with the Yorkshire County Cricket Club and the MCC. The Hall is probably best known as the childhood home of the Duchess of Kent, who was married from here in York Minster. The house may be visited by parties (by appointment) in the summer.

The village has many Georgian houses, a green, a stream and tree-lined lanes. The tower of the mainly-Victorian church, *All Saints'*, and the W doorway date from Anglo-Saxon times, while a carved slab of *c*.800 is among remains of the pre-Norman period to be seen in the church.

### Howardian Hills C2/C3
*Ryedale. Between A19 & A64*

This range of low, cultivated hills extends from the neighbourhood of Coxwold in the W to the River Derwent E of Malton, and forms the high ground between the Vale of Pickering and the Plain of York. The Howardians are separated from the steeper *Hambleton* range, which continues NW, on the N side of the Gilling Gap through which the Holbeck flows E on its way to meet the River Rye. On their E they are separated from the Yorkshire Wolds by the River Derwent which flows S past Malton through the Kirkham Gorge to the Plain of York.

Rising no higher than 565ft, these gentle undulating hills were formed through a series of faults in the Corallian limestone.

### Hubberholme A2
*Wharfedale. Village on B6160. 18m N of Skipton*

Hubberholme at the head of Wharfedale is a riverside village with a lovely little church situated on one side of the bridge, and *The George Inn* on the other. The **Church of St Michael and All Angels** is first mentioned in records dated 1241, when it was dedicated to St Oswald as a forest chapel for the monks of Coverham Abbey (near *East Witton*) by William de Percy, Lord of the Manor. The most interesting feature is the oak rood loft, the only other in Yorkshire being at Flamborough. This one, dated 1558, bears an inscription and an amulet and the Percy badge.

The *carvings* on the chairs, choir stalls and pews, made in 1934, bear testimony to the skill of Robert Thompson of *Kilburn*, whose mouse device is there for the seeking. A cracked bell, dated 1601, bears the arms of Elizabeth I. The *Lewis Window* depicts the regular experience of luckless curates who had to cross Horse Head Moor from the village of *Halton Gill* (SW) to take services. Halton Gill lies at the lonely head of *Littondale*, and both villages once had chapels-of-ease within the parish of *Arncliffe*, lower down Littondale. One such hapless individual wrote in 1743: 'In the winter quarter it is with great danger and difficulty I pass over very high mountains and large drifts of snow to the chapel'.

*The George Inn* was once the vicarage, and it remained church property until 1965. It is the scene each New Year's Eve of an unusual ceremony in which the villagers foregather to bid for the tenancy of a 16-acre field, bequeathed in trust for the poor of the parish. The Vicar accompanied by the churchwardens auctions the tenancy; a candle decides the length of the auction, which lasts until the flame expires. The last bidder is then declared tenant of the field. Proceeds go to pensioners.

The *Dalesway long-distance walk passes near the village.

## Hutton-le-Hole                                    C2

*Ryedale. Village off A170, 2m N of Kirkbymoorside*

Arguably the most beautiful village in Yorkshire, Hutton-le-Hole is divided by a fast-flowing beck rushing down from Spaunton Moor. There is a wide, undulating green on both banks of the beck, which is spanned by a number of white-painted footbridges; old, red-roofed stone cottages are scattered in disordered fashion at the back of the green, with the occasional café or shop. Tourism is big business here during the season.

Apart from its beauty, the village's main attraction is the **Ryedale Folk Museum** which occupies a site of some 2 acres. The life and work of an agricultural community from the 16th c. is demonstrated by collections of domestic hardware and furniture, with tools of varying 19th-c. crafts. There are prehistoric flint implements, and Romano-British artefacts and pottery. Behind the museum is a park in which a 16th-c. cruck-framed house has been reconstructed.

Other reconstructed buildings include a 16th-c. manor house and glass furnace, an 18th-c. cottage, a 19th-c. blacksmith's shop and crofter's cottage, barn and wheelshed. There is also a wagon park.

## Ilkley                                            B3

*Wharfedale. Pop 13,058. 9m SE of Skipton (A65). Events: Literature Festival (biennial); Wharfedale Music Festival (2nd & 3rd week in May); Ballet Seminar (Jul/Aug); Open Lawn Tennis Tournament (early Aug). EC Wed. Inf: Tel (0943) 602319*

This town of broad, tree-lined avenues stands at the N edge of Ilkley Moor, widely known through the comic song. The town, however, was formerly an elegant Victorian spa and now serves as a dormitory town for Bradford and Leeds, as a retirement haven and as a tourist and shopping centre with annual arts festivals. It is at the terminus of the Leeds and Bradford railways and is divided by the River Wharfe which is crossed by three bridges, the oldest being a buttressed, high *saddle-back bridge* with three arches, built over three centuries ago and now used only by pedestrians. The Yorkshire end of the *Dalesway long-distance walk joins the *Ebor Way at Ilkley.

The new, residential part of the town,

occupying the N or Middleton bank of the river, has most of the district's sporting facilities. The older part of the town, the commercial centre, is on the S bank.

**All Saints' Church**, founded in 627, occupies a site on the vanished Roman settlement of Olicana which commanded a cross-roads connecting Aldborough with Manchester, and Ribchester with York. Most of the church dates from the 1860s, but the S doorway is 13th-c. and the tower 15th-c. The enclosed pew, dated 1633, and five oak pew doors, are survivors of the old seating arrangements. There are two Roman altars, and, most interesting of all, three carved Anglo-Saxon crosses, believed to date from the 8th c. They stand in the tower with special lighting and description boards, surrounded by shields of notabilities connected with the church and surrounding district.

Adjoining the church is the fine 16th-c. *Manor House*, now the **Museum and Art Gallery**, with displays of local Roman and prehistoric finds. Bronze Age *cup-and-ring* markings can be seen in *Gardens* near the town centre.

On the moortop escarpment to the SE of Ilkley are the millstone grit formations of the **Cow and Calf Rocks**. There are fine views over Wharfedale from here. Further W **White Wells**, a whitewashed stone building dating from 1756, houses a pair of circular *plunge baths* in the basement; they are fed by a spring, having been cut from the bedrock, and are often erroneously thought to be Roman. Part of the building serves as an exhibition centre for the Wharfedale Naturalists' Society during the season, and refreshments can be obtained. Between White Wells and the town is a tarn with wildfowl, around which a pleasant walk gives good views of moor and valley. 1m S of White Wells is a fine Bronze Age stone circle known as the *Twelve Apostles*.

Also on the moor, SW of the town, the mysterious **Swastika Stone**, enclosed by railings, can be seen just beyond the woodlands of *Heber's Ghyll*. Incised with a primitive religious symbol, the stone is thought to date from the Iron Age or earlier. Only two similar stones are known, in Greece and Sweden.

On the Middleton side of the river is the *Middleton Lodge* retreat of the Passionist Fathers, with Stations of the Cross and a Calvary in the grounds; *Middleton Woods* are especially attractive in spring, carpeted with bluebells. Details of *Nature Trails* around the town are available from the Wharfedale Naturalists' Society.

2m NE, set in splendid parkland, is one of John Carr's finest mansions, *Denton Hall*, rebuilt by him in the 1770s. Thomas, 3rd Baron Fairfax of Cameron, was born here in an earlier house; he distinguished himself at the Battle of *Marston Moor* in 1644 and was appointed Supreme Commander the following year.

### Ingleton
A2

*Ribblesdale. Town on A65/B6255, 11m NW of Settle. Inf: (0468) 41049/41280. Nat Park Inf (Clapham): Tel (04685) 419*

Set beneath the S point of Whernside, Ingleton with its neighbour **Clapham** (5m SE) is the pot-holing, rock climbing and fell walking centre for W Craven. Founded on coal, it later thrived on quarrying, cotton and lime and has been popular with tourists since the Skipton railway was built in 1849. N of the town are *Thornton Force*, *Pecca Falls* and *Snow Falls*, all accessible on foot. Thornton Force drops 40ft into a rock-girt pool in a beautiful glen. It is possible to walk along a rock ledge behind the force.

Favourite walks follow the remote valleys of the Twiss and the Doe; the B6255 leads NE between Whernside and Ingleborough towards Wharfedale, while a route along beautiful *Kingsdale* on Whernside's W flank leads to Dentdale in Cumbria. *Whernside*, at 2419ft North Yorkshire's highest peak, gives good views into Cumbria from its summit. S is the characteristic long, low but rugged form of *Ingleborough*.

This is the most popular of *Craven's* millstone-grit-capped 'three peaks'; a walk from Clapham towards Ingleborough's SE spur passes **Ingleborough Cave**, a great cavern with stalactites and stalagmites which can be followed for almost 1000ft, and the famous swallow-hole **Gaping Gill**. The Brigantian tribe are said to have had a settlement on this windswept hill; Iron Age people built a fort here. Low down on the SW slopes by the B6255 (about 2m from Ingleton) are the **White Scar Caves**, showpieces since the 1920s.

At the head of the Doe valley between Whernside and Ingleborough is the village of *Chapel le Dale*; from the old *Hill Inn* a route can be taken to *Southerscales Farm*, beneath the NW slope of Ingleborough. Here, the *Southerscales Nature Reserve* is managed by the Royal Society for Nature Conservation. Visitors can see excellent examples of limestone pavement formations with characteristic flowers and ferns which flourish in the sheltered and humid fissures (known as 'grikes'). The slopes of the hill above the farm have a series of pot-holes.

*Ingleborough Hall* at Clapham is the former home of the botanist Reginald Farrer, and there is a *Nature Trail* named after him. The grounds have a lake.

### Jervaulx Abbey
B2

*Wensleydale. Off A6108, 3m SE of Middleham*

The Cistercian Abbey of Jervaulx was founded in 1156, and in its heyday held all the dale's land up-river as far as its source. Ruined since the Pilgrimage of Grace in which the last Abbot took part and for which he was executed (1537), the insubstantial remains occupy a charming site of trees, grasses and wild flowers.

Little remains of the church, but from it the principal remaining structures can be seen. These are the Early English *Chapter House* (with two windows flanking the entrance still intact), the *Cloister* and sections of the *Kitchen* and *Refectory*, with fireplaces and ovens. The dominant feature is a lofty wall of the *Dormitory*, originally 180ft long, with a line of lancet windows. The site is privately owned.

### Keld
A2

*Swaledale. Village off B6270, 11m SE of Kirkby Stephen*

This is a village of cottages clustered round a little square where East Gill, tumbling down from Rogan's Seat, joins the parent Swale. It is the village furthest up-dale, surrounded by high, wild fells. The river and the dale road part company here: each leads S to skirt *Kisdon Hill*, the river on the E flank and the road on the W. In early times when the parish church down-dale at *Grinton* had the nearest burial ground, 'Corpse Way' led over Kisdon Hill.

Keld is an ideal centre for hikers. The *Pennine Way* crosses Stonesdale Moor, following the beck and twisting moorland road as the route goes N to Tan Hill: here in the 19th c. coal was mined, and on the surrounding moorlands the hardy Swaledale sheep were first bred. At 1732ft, *Tan Hill Inn* is the highest in England.

Near the village is a spectacular group of waterfalls, of which **Kisdon Force** is the most attractive, a beautiful triple fall rushing over rocky shelves into a romantic glen walled in by high, wooded cliffs. *Wain Wath Falls* can be seen from the dale road which continues W from Keld along Birkdale towards Kirkby Stephen; *Catrake Force* and *Currack Force* are also accessible from the village. Potholers favour the surrounding fells, whose limestone sides are riddled with subterranean passages of varying difficulty.

**Kettlewell** A3
*Wharfedale. Village on B6160, 15m N of Skipton. EC Tue, Thur*

Since the closure of the lead mines and the corn, cotton and smelt mills, as well as the railway at Grassington in 1902, the commercial activity of the village has waned. It now relies on tourism for its prosperity, and during the holiday season crowds throng its attractive, narrow lanes.

In *St Mary's* churchyard the author Charles John Cutcliffe Hyne is buried. After settling in the village as a writer of adventure stories, he became famous as the creator of 'Captain Kettle'.

Just outside the village on the Conistone road, high above the river, is *Scargill House*, a Church of England conference centre and retreat opened in 1959 by the Bradford Diocese. When seen from a distance the buildings – especially the *Chapel* of 1961 silhouetted against pine trees – might give a stranger the impression of passing through a Swiss canton rather than a Yorkshire dale.

A lonely gated road from here climbs precipitously E of Cam Head to *\*Coverdale* and passes *Great Whernside*, a long, flat-topped hill reaching 2310ft. The B6160 follows Wharfedale to Kidstones Pass, Bishopdale, and thence to the W end of Wensleydale.

**Kilburn** C2
*N Yorks. Village off A170, 6m SE of Thirsk*

Kilburn is situated in the Gilling Gap which separates the Hambleton and Howardian Hills. A charming village with a bridge-spanned stream running beside the main street, it has become widely known through the superb craftsmanship of Robert Thompson, the woodcarver. Born and bred in the village, Thompson set up a carving centre here, using local craftsmen. The firm has a mouse symbol as its trademark. Thompson died in 1955, and since then the business has been continued by his grandsons and a fine team of craftsmen. The *showrooms* are housed in a picturesque half-timbered Elizabethan house, and are a considerable tourist attraction.

The village is overlooked from the N by the **White Horse of Kilburn**, a gigantic turf-cut figure (314ft by 228ft) near *Roulston Scar*. Periodically restored with chalk from the Yorkshire Wolds, it was made in 1857 between October 28 and November 4, by the village schoolmaster, **John Hodgson**, and 32 villagers, at the behest of **Thomas Taylor**, a local man who had made his fortune as a London merchant. The horse can be seen for

miles around, and has magnificent views over the *Plain of York*.

The horse is reached from **Kilburn** along the Oldstead road; a left turn ascends by way of the *White Horse Road*. On a clear day, the 200ft climb up a series of steps beside the horse rewards with a patchwork view as far as the Pennines. This spur of the *\*Cleveland Way* starts from *\*Sutton Bank*, N.

White Horse walks pass through the Hambleton Forest area, which belongs to the Forestry Commission. The Horse itself is maintained by the Kilburn White Horse Association.

**Kilnsey** A3
*Wharfedale. Village on B6160, 4m NW of Grassington*

Set on the W bank of the River Wharfe, the village is overshadowed by the massive bulk of **Kilnsey Crag**, a great limestone outcrop left here after the Ice Age. Each year in summer, races staged between the water meadows and the crag test fitness as well as speed; the crag also provides a challenge for rock climbers, who can sometimes be seen attempting to scale its treacherous overhanging face.

Just before the crag is reached on the Kettlewell road from Grassington, further down-dale, is the **Kilnsey Park and Trout Farm** where visitors can see a fresh-water aquarium and trout-feeding ponds, and purchase fresh or smoked farm produce. There are picnic areas in the grounds. The walk from Kilnsey to *Malhamdale*, along Mastiles Lane, has splendid views.

**Kiplin Hall** see *Bolton-on-Swale*

**Kirby Misperton** see *Pickering*

**Kirkby Malham** A3
*Malhamdale (Airedale). Village off A65, 10m NW of Skipton*

This Malhamdale village is on Kirkby Beck, just before it joins the Aire. The **Church of St Michael the Archangel** has a memorial to John Lambert (1619-84). Known as 'Honest John' because of his fair-mindedness and fearless honesty, Lambert was born in nearby Calton. In the Civil War he led Fairfax's cavalry at Marston Moor, and subsequently became Commissary-General and a Major-General. He later took part in the battles of Preston and Worcester, captured Pontefract Castle, and participated in the overthrow of Richard Cromwell. Following his capture and trial after the Restoration he ended his days in prison on Drake's Island in Plymouth Sound.

Another memorial, to Walter Morrison of Malham, is the beautiful sanctuary panelling carved in 1923. It is enriched by 16 colourful shields. Other items of interest include the Jacobean altar rail, handsome Georgian box pews and a 12th-c. font which was found in the churchyard, abandoned but undamaged. The church bells were those heard by Tom, the chimney sweep, on his way to the river in Kingsley's *The Water Babies*, which was partly written at *Malham*.

From this lovely village there is a footpath leading beside the beck to Malham, 1m N; the road to Settle in Ribblesdale has some magnificent views.

## Kirkbymoorside     C2

*Ryedale. Town on A170, 6m E of Helmsley. EC Thur MD Wed*

A bypass on the S now syphons off through-traffic that once caused congestion in the summer season, and separates the old, attractive market town from a modern industrial estate.

The cobble-edged market place with its old-fashioned shops and ancient hostelries has an interesting *Tolbooth* (also known as Market Hall, or Memorial Hall). It was built (*c.* 1700) of stone quarried from a 16th-c. castle which once stood on Vivers Hill, at the top of Castlegate. The Tolbooth's ground floor is used as a covered market, and the upper floor as a meeting hall. Opposite is '*Buckingham House*' where Charles II's fallen favourite, the licentious George Villiers, 2nd Duke of Buckingham, died in 1687. The building was then probably part of the adjoining *King's Head Hotel*. Also in the Market Place is the part-timbered 17th-c. *Black Swan Inn*, once a staging post for the York coach.

Several streets branching off the market place reward a stroll with their quiet charm. Behind the Tolbooth is a market cross and *The Shambles*, a narrow cobbled street with shuttered shops dating from the 17th c. Near Vivers Hill is **All Saints' Church**, extensively restored in 1873-5, but still retaining much medieval flavour. The two-storey porch dates from the 15th c. Behind the church a path leads to *Vivers Hill*, where the moat and fishponds are all that remain of a 12th-c. castle built by the Stuteville family. Nearby, some foundation stones and sections of rubble walling show the site of the later castle, built by Charles Neville, 6th Earl of Westmorland.

Kirkbymoorside's brass band, famous for miles around, tours the area in summer to play at carnivals, fêtes and country shows.

Visitors find the town itself a good centre for touring two of Ryedale's prettiest dales, which lie to either side: *\*Farndale*, and *Kirk Dale* below *\*Bransdale*. *Hodge Beck* in Kirk Dale is forded just N of the A170, near the quarry-site *cave* in which were discovered the bones of prehistoric beasts in 1821 – elephant, hyena, tiger, bear and wolf. The cave is rather inaccessible, and is best viewed from the floor of the quarry by which it is approached.

Higher up the beck and standing solitary at the mouth of a wooded glen is **St Gregory's Minster**, a tiny late Anglo-Saxon church with Norman and 15th-c. work and Victorian rebuilding. Its tower dates from 1827. The chancel arch is of the same period as a sundial over the porch, *c.* 1060, which bears a lengthy inscription in Northumbrian English commemorating the purchase of the ruined minster and its rebuilding by Orm, son of Gamal. Two *stone slabs* are claimed to cover the graves of King Ethelwald and Bishop Cedd; although the authenticity of this claim has been challenged (there is little doubt that Bishop Cedd rests in the church at *\*Lastingham*), the age and beauty of the carved coverings cannot be denied. They are thought to date from the 9th and 11th c.

## Kirk Dale see *Kirkbymoorside*

## Kirkham Priory     C3

*N Yorks. Off A64, 5m SW of Malton*

The priory stands in a charming setting of river, meadows, hills and woodlands beside an old stone bridge in the *Kirkham Gorge*, where the River Derwent flows through one of the prettiest sections of its course. An Augustinian house, the priory was founded in the 12th c. by Walter L'Espec.

The priory's 13th-c. *Gatehouse* has carvings of heraldic shields among its elaborate sculptures, and is the largest remaining fragment of the ruins; also notable is the Romanesque *doorway* of the refectory, and the fine 13th-c. *Lavatorium*, or monk's washing place, in the cloiser.

## Knaresborough     B3

*Nidderdale. Pop 11,780. 3m NE of Harrogate (A59/A6055, B6163/B6164/B6165). Event: Bed Race (Jun). EC Thur MD Wed. Inf: Tel (0423) 866886*

Knaresborough is spectacularly sited on a deep wooded gorge carved out of the limestone by the River Nidd. A jumble of old houses and gardens, cafés, shops and inns clings to the precipitous N bank, the whole topped off by the castle standing on a rocky crag above the water. The gorge is crossed by the *High Bridge* and the *Low Bridge* (both old bridges enlarged in the 18th c.) and the high-arched railway viaduct carrying the line between Harrogate and York. Boating is available on the river in summer.

The town has a wealth of elegant 18th-c. houses and shop fronts. Along the top of the town the High Street runs parallel to the river below, and here *Knaresborough House*, a late 18th-c. mansion, overlooks the spacious churchyard on its N side. In the handsome market place near Kirkgate one of the period shops claims to be the oldest *Chemist's Shop* in England (1720).

Near the market place is the Norman **Castle**, of which little remains apart from its ruined 14th-c. keep. It was to this retreat that Henry II's four knights fled after their murder of Thomas à Becket in Canterbury Cathedral. In the Middle Ages the castle had many royal associations: Richard II was kept prisoner here before being transferred to Pontefract, where he was murdered (1400). The dungeon (the 'King's Chamber') is hewn out of the solid rock. There is a small *Museum* on the ground floor of the keep; near the entrance, the **Old Court House Museum** has local history displays. The building was once the court house of Knaresborough's Forest Court.

From its commanding position the castle has a magnificent view of the gorge and of the *Church of St John the Baptist* with its central tower and spirelet, situated halfway up the steep hillside. The church was built between the 12th and 14th c. and partly rebuilt in the 15th c., and holds monuments to the Slingsby family.

A curiosity near Abbey Road and Low Bridge is a house of three storeys (*The House in the Rock*) hewn out of the solid rocky hillside by a Knaresborough weaver between 1770 and 1786. The house is also known as *Fort Montague*, after the family name of the Dukes of Buccleuch; it was visited by the Duchess during its construction. On the limestone cliffs by the river are some interesting sites. Just below The House in the Rock is the early 15th-c. *Chapel of Our Lady of the Crag* (or *St Robert's Chapel*), hewn 10ft deep in the rock, a fine example of a wayside shrine. A carved figure of a Knight Templar, wearing armour and drawing his sword, stands at the entrance; inside can be seen a statue of the Virgin and Child, an altar, bench and pair of piscinas, and four grotesquely-carved anonymous faces. Almost 1m downstream is a grotto known as *St Robert's Cave*, the saint's hermitage. It was here that the notorious murderer Eugene

Aram, born in *Ramsgill, buried his victim Daniel Clark (1745).

Above Low Bridge on the right bank of the Nidd, close to the *cave* where Mother Shipton was born, is the **Dropping Well**; here the water falls over an overhanging rock from which hang various objects placed there to be petrified. This process takes anything from a few months to a couple of years, and results from the effects of chlorides, lime, magnesia and sulphates in the water which gradually coat any object in a brownish, rock-hard shell. Gloves, hats, stockings and toys are the commonest objects left here, but anything else will do. No less phenomenal, perhaps, were the remarkable prophesies made by Mother Shipton in the 1500s, some of which have come to pass, although she was inaccurate in her prediction that 'The world to an end will come in eighteen hundred and eighty one'. Apart from Mother Shipton, the town's best-known character was John (Blind Jack) Metcalfe, born in 1717 and blinded by smallpox at the age of six: musician, soldier, sportsman, and England's first major road builder, he died at the age of 93.

Up-river towards High Bridge is the Elizabethan *Old Manor House*, gabled and half-timbered. Its chequerboard appearance marks it out from a distance. Near High Bridge is *Conyngham Hall*, an 18th-c. mansion with **Grounds** laid out as a park and zoo.

**Lastingham**                                  C2
*Ryedale. Village off A170, 4m NE of Kirkbymoorside*
This attractive village lies sheltered at the edge of Spaunton Moor away from the main stream of traffic. The old stone cottages are scattered around the green; the white timber fencing, and footbridges crossing Hole Beck, add to their charm. The stone *bridge* is inscribed with the name of John Jackson, an artist who gave it to his home village. There is a hotel, and a 17th-c. inn stands opposite the church, which was a priory in early Norman times. Before the Benedictine monks moved to *York, to found St Mary's Abbey (*c.* 1087), their intention had been to erect 'a great church at Lestingau'. This was never fulfilled, but they left behind one of the area's most delightful ecclesiastical buildings.

**St Mary's Church** stands on the site of a monastery founded in 654 by St Cedd. He is buried in the early Norman *crypt*, which was built as his shrine and is one of Yorkshire's ecclesiastical treasures: it is vaulted, with massive columns and a semi-circular apse at the N end. It has the head of a great

Anglo-Saxon cross (c. 8th c.), and other relics of pre-Norman times. The church dates from 1078; the tower is 15th c., and the Victorian restoration was the sensitive work of J. L. Pearson (1879). The building is a worthy reminder of the medieval period when St Mary's was considered one of Northumbria's most sacred sites, and was a notable place of pilgrimage.

Other Anglo-Saxon relics are to be seen in the tiny dale church, St Gregory's Minster, near *Kirkbymoorside.

### Levisham                                      C2
N Yorks. Village off A169, 5m NE of Pickering

'Melton Carbury' of Brideshead Revisited, Levisham is a remote place with a green overlooking a narrow valley beneath Levisham Moor.

Levisham Station in *Newton Dale (W) is the first halt on the *North Yorkshire Moors Railway which follows the original Pickering-Whitby track for 18m N as far as Grosmont in Esk Dale. From Newtondale Halt, further along the track, the Forestry Commission has laid out some forest walks through Cropton Forest, which borders the line on its W. The longest walk (7m) is to Levisham Station. The rail line passes Levisham Moor on its E and the ruin of Skelton Tower, built in the mid-19th c. by the Rev. Robert Skelton of Levisham as a peaceful retreat.

Levisham Moor stretching N from the village is rich in prehistoric earthworks and tumuli, excavated by the Scarborough Archaeological Society. Footpaths lead across the moor to the phenomenal hollow, the *Hole of Horcum, due N of Levisham, where Levisham Beck has its source.

### Leyburn                                       B2
Wensleydale. Town on A684/A6108, 11m SW of Richmond. EC Wed MD Fri. Inf: Tel (0969) 23069

Leyburn stands on high ground N of the River Ure. The town has a variety of good shops strung around a large, sloping central square: this is a hive of activity on market days, since Leyburn is the trading centre for farming communities from a large area. The Chandler Gallery in Commercial Square has changing exhibitions, and a craft shop.

On its route S to Middleham the A6108 crosses the river by a single-lane bridge, formerly a toll bridge (the old toll house still stands). This ornate construction of iron slung between pseudo-medieval towers would seem better suited to an industrial setting than to its rural surroundings of rolling pastureland in lower Wensleydale.

3m E of Leyburn is **Constable Burton Hall**, a mid-Georgian house designed by John Carr of York which contains fine paintings, a unique collection of Chippendale furniture and one of Yorkshire's finest model railways. The Gardens have woodlands and alpines.

To the N of the town stretches a wooded limestone scar known as 'The Shawl', which affords delightful walks and splendid views over the lower dale. Mary, Queen of Scots is said to have been recaptured here in an escape attempt during her imprisonment in *Bolton Castle, up-dale.

### Lightwater Valley see Ripon

### Linton                                        A3
Wharfedale. Village on B6265, 7m N of Skipton

The green is divided by Linton Beck with its packhorse and clapper bridges; the village is surrounded by trees. Fountaine's Hospital, standing at one end of the green, is quite divorced from traditional Dales' architecture; endowed as almshouses by Richard Fountaine in 1721, it was designed in the style of Vanbrugh and has a central block with a cupola over a Venetian window and an arched doorway.

The Church of St Michael and All Angels, ½m E, stands by the River Wharfe close to a weir and to a turbulent stretch of water flowing through a fault in the limestone. Stepping stones near here lead to a path for *Grassington, less than 1m N. The church dates from the 14th c., but has Norman touches inside.

The novelist Halliwell Sutcliffe once lived here, as does Dr Arthur Raistrick who has written many books on the history, industry and traditions of the Dales.

### Little Ribston                                B3
Nidderdale. Village on B6164, 4m SE of Knaresborough

This village achieved fame in 1709, when the first Ribston Pippin apple was raised in England in the Hall grounds. Three seeds were brought from Normandy but only one germinated; from that single seed countless orchards materialised, and the Cox's Orange Pippin was developed. The original tree was blown down many years ago, but the stump remains.

### Lofthouse                                     B2
Nidderdale. Village off B6265, 7m NW of Pateley Bridge

Situated between Scar House and Gouthwaite Reservoirs in the high reaches of *Nidderdale, Lofthouse lies close to remote roads and panoramic views. Just below the village How Stean Beck, flowing from Conistone Moor (W), joins the Nidd: the beck passes through fossil limestone at **How Stean Gorge**, a narrow chasm with a marble-like rock bed worn into shelves, reaching its greatest depth at about 70ft. Privately owned and open to the public, the gorge is crossed by rustic bridges enabling visitors to climb from the water's edge past caves and waterfalls to fenced-off galleries in the cliff-face, high above the stream. There are picnic spots, refreshments and a children's play area.

The gorge is reached by a lane leading W: above the bridge the single-track Waterworks Toll Road skirts the hillside and arrives at *Scar House* and *Angram Reservoirs* near Little Whernside. This is wild, impressive and lonely country, riddled with pot-holes; the road has stopping places and some picnic areas, one situated near *Goyden Pot*. 300 yds N, the river rushes into *Manchester Hole* and continues its course underground, reappearing 2m S at *Nidd Heads* near Lofthouse. 1m NW of the village is *Middlesmoor*, an ancient settlement almost 1000ft above sea level, with views from the churchyard that extend down-dale across Gouthwaite Reservoir and *Ramsgill* to Pateley Bridge.

## Lyke Wake Walk                                    C2/D2
*N Yorks. Long-distance footpath*

The walk follows a 40m route across the North Yorkshire Moors between *Osmotherley* (W) and *Ravenscar* on the coast, the stretch between Osmotherley and Cockayne Head on Bransdale Moor following the *Cleveland Way*. This passes the Cleveland Forest's *Clay Bank* picnic area on the B1257, here crossing the top of *Bilsdale* and the highest point of the Cleveland Hills, *Botton Head* on Urra Moor (1490ft).

The walk was established by Bill Cowley in 1955, and is now the most popular on the Moors. The name recalls the ancient practice of 'waking', or keeping vigil over a dead body ('lyke'). In early days those completing the route within 24 hrs qualified for membership of the Lyke Wake Club, and were rewarded with a certificate and a badge in the shape of a coffin.

The route crosses some of the loneliest stretches of the moors, encountering numerous prehistoric sites, and following ancient tracks of miners, smugglers and monks. It crosses the Roman road, 'Wade's Causeway' (see *Cawthorn Roman Camps*) on Wheeldale Moor, then by contrast encounters the *North Yorkshire Moors*

*Railway* before passing the Fylingdales Early Warning Station (see also *Goathland*). The last leg of its journey takes walkers to the coast at *Ravenscar*.

Recently the tourist authorities have shown concern over the extensive erosion caused by walkers on the route.

## Malham                                              A3
*Malhamdale. Village off A65, 11m NW of Skipton. Nat Park Inf: Tel (07293) 363*

Situated near the head of Malhamdale at the source of the river, Malham is a pleasant little place with the infant Aire running under hump-backed *Monks Bridge*, and houses clustered around the green. High above the village the river rises deep underground in the limestone above Malham Tarn and is not visible until it leaves the Tarn. It disappears again a little way S, re-emerging as a sparkling stream from Malham Cove N of the village. The area around Malham has some of the wildest limestone, fell and moorland scenery in England: a great attraction for the numerous tourists who flood the village at the height of the holiday season.

**Malham Cove** is a magnificent 250ft-high curving limestone wall, part of the Craven Fault stretching 22m from Wharfedale to Kirkby Lonsdale in Cumbria. Further N (2¼m from the village) is **Malham Tarn**, a 150-acre natural lake. The lake and much of the surrounding country are owned by the National Trust: *Malham Tarn House* is leased by the Trust to the Field Studies Council, which holds regular courses relating to conservation and the scientific study of the countryside in all its aspects. The *limestone pavement* between the Tarn and Malham Cove is highly valued as a botanists' study site. The *Pennine Way* N through Malhamdale crosses the pavement to the tarn, having passed through Malham. (See *Walks*, p. 22.)

It was at Tarn House that Charles Kingsley began writing *The Water Babies*: Kingsley was a friend of the owner, Walter Morrison – the 'Sir John Harthover' of the book. It was at this house, too, that Tom the chimney sweep was surprised to see his reflection in a mirror, and the church bells he heard on his way to the river were those of *Kirkby Malham*. The valley and surrounding hills all featured in the story.

E of Malham Tarn, Gordale Beck flows down from the tops to join the Aire: on its way it plunges in a spectacular fall over **Gordale Scar**. This 300ft ravine, caused by the collapse of a subterranean cavern roof, can be approached by road from Malham (1½m).

**Malhamdale** see *Airedale & Malhamdale*

**Malton** C3
*Ryedale. Town on B1248/B1257, 8m S of Pickering.
EC Thur MD Sat*

'Capital' of Ryedale, Malton stands at the E
edge of the Howardian Hills on the River
Derwent, which here enters the Kirkham
Gorge from the *Vale of Pickering*. The town
is on the railway connecting York with
Scarborough, and at a meeting of roads from
the Vale, the Plain of York and the Yorkshire
Wolds. At the centre of Ryedale's
agricultural district, it has England's third
largest cattle market. In spring, the town's
roadside verges are brightened by thousands
of daffodils.

Many relics of the Roman fortified town of
Derventio have been unearthed, and most
are displayed in the Town Hall **Museum**.
Built in the 18th c., the *Town Hall* stands in
the market place close to the 12th-c. *St
Michael's Church*, which occupies an island
site. A predominantly Norman church
with a 15th-c. tower, it has some 19th-c.
restoration work. Its modern stained glass
depicts diocesan and manorial heraldry. On
Church Hill, *St Leonard's Church* with its
Perpendicular tower and 19th-c. spire has
an amusing brass plate to a local iron-founder
(*d.* 1837), showing him at drink and at
prayer.

Many of the town's old inns and houses
survive, some of the inns being close to three
centuries old. *The Talbot Hotel* in
Yorkersgate was converted from a hunting
lodge (*c.* 1740) 'to accommodate travellers of
fashion'; in Wheelgate the 18th-c. *Cross Keys*
has been built over a Norman stone-vaulted
crypt which is now part of the inn's cellar,
but was at one time a priory rest-house.

Straddling the Pickering road just N of the
Roman fort site and 1m outside the town is
*Old Malton*, a pleasant place of old
stone-and-tiled houses and quaint cottages.
It is dominated by the 12th-c. parish church,
**St Mary's**, which occupies the surviving
nave of a Gilbertine priory and has a superb
Early English *W front*. The Norman arcading
of the nave embedded in the walls is a legacy
of the removal of the aisles and clerestory and
the resulting enclosure of the nave. It is the
last Gilbertine priory in England to be used as
a place of worship.

Malton is well known as a racehorse
training area, and many winners have come
out of the local racing stables.

**Markenfield Hall** see *Ripon*

**Marrick Priory** see *Reeth*

**Marske** B2
*Swaledale. Village off A6108, 5m W of Richmond*

Marske is situated on the beck of the same
name just above its meeting with the River
Swale. The turbulent beck flows under a
15th-c. ribbed arched *bridge* and through the
estate of 18th-c. *Marske Hall*, overlooked by
a 60ft *obelisk* raised in memory of Captain
Matthew Hutton, whose family's connection
with the estate goes back to 1598. The
Hutton family produced two Archbishops of
York, one going on to Canterbury in 1757.
Adjoining the bridge is **St Edmund's
Church**, of Norman origin but restored in
1683, with a double-decker pulpit, box pews,
and the Hutton shield over the porch.

**Marston Moor** C3
*Nidderdale. Battle site off B1224, 7m W of York*

Marston Moor is flat and fertile farmland
with great skyscapes and far distant views of
York, and of the Wolds and the North
Yorkshire hills beyond. The Battle of
Marston Moor was centred N of the short
stretch of road connecting the villages of
*Long Marston* (SE) and *Tockwith* (NW); a
stone **obelisk** by the road commemorates the
event.

On 2nd July 1644 the Parliamentarians led
by Oliver Cromwell and Sir Thomas Fairfax
sought to defend their siege of York against
the forces of Prince Rupert of the Rhine,
nephew of Charles I. Some 50,000 men
joined battle, and of these about 4000
Royalists and 300 Parliamentarians were
killed in three hours of fighting. The rout of
Prince Rupert's forces sealed the ultimate
fate of the Royalist cause.

**Masham** B2
*N Yorks. Town on A6108, 9m NW of Ripon. Event:
Steam Engine & Fair Organ Rally (Jun). EC Thur
MD Wed*

Masham (pronounced 'Masm') stands just N
of the confluence of the Rivers Ure and Burn.
Not strictly in Wensleydale, it has the feel of
a lower dale town, with pastoral hilly country
around. The town has a large, French-style
market square with a tree-shaped cross,
bordered by elegant houses and shops. The
town's charter was granted in 1250.

Dominating the square is the largely
Victorian church, **St Mary's**, whose
Norman tower was topped with a tall spire in
the 15th c. Inside there are some interesting
monuments, and over the chancel arch is a
large painting by Reynolds of the upper
portion of Christ's Nativity. Damaged by fire
at Belvoir Castle in 1816, the surviving piece
got to Masham – it is not known how. The
church's most treasured possession is the

carved shaft of an Anglo-Saxon cross, dating from the early 9th c. The much-weathered carving represents the Adoration of the Magi and the 12 Apostles. The cross stands in the churchyard.

Just out of town is *Swinton Park*, an early 18th-c. mansion enlarged by James Wyatt *c*. 1800 and extravagantly redesigned in 1821. The house is now owned by Lindley Lodge, a Christian educational trust which provides conference facilities and training for young people. In one of the towers is a 17th-c. single-handed clock known as a 'cage-striking' clock because its mechanism is enclosed within a birdcage-like structure. Beyond the park at *Ilton* (about 2m SW) is a folly known as the *Druid's Temple*, a replica of Stonehenge, created in the 1820s.

## Middleham                                        B2
*Wensleydale. Village on A6108, 2m SE of Leyburn. EC Thur*

Situated between the River Ure and the River Cover (which meet about 1m E), Middleham is a grey, sloping Dales town dominated by its huge ruined Dales **Castle**. Founded in the 11th c. to guard the route between Richmond and Skipton, the castle passed in the 13th c. to the Neville family. Richard Neville, Earl of Warwick – 'The Kingmaker' – held Edward IV prisoner in the castle during the Wars of the Roses.

After Warwick's death the king's brother, later Richard III, was granted the castle; he married Warwick's daughter Anne, and their only son Edward was born and died here (1473-84). During the Civil War the Parliamentarians ordered the dismantling of the castle, and thereafter it fell gradually into ruin. Its massive gritstone walls and vast scale have preserved it from complete disintegration; the keep stands almost to its original height; and much remains to remind us of its greatest period in the 15th c. when it was centre of government for the North of England, and provided Shakespeare with part of the setting for *Henry VI*.

In the 14th-c. *Church of St Mary and St Alkelda* is a window given in 1934 by the Richard III Society in memory of the king. Also associated with Richard is the *Swire Cross* in the market square, thought to have been put up to commemorate the granting to Middleham by Richard of a twice yearly fair and market.

The village, once an important market and a administrative centre for **Wensleydale**, has some fine buildings of varying styles dating from the 17th c; its famous racing and breeding stables are said to have been first introduced by the monks from Jervaulx. On most days, thoroughbreds can be seen training on Middleham Moor.

**Mount Grace Priory** see *Osmotherley*

**Muker** see *Thwaite*

**Newburgh Priory** see *Coxwold*

## Newby Hall (Skelton)                             B3
*Nidderdale. Historic house off B6265, 4m SE of Ripon*

The Hall was begun in the 1690s, but Robert Adam created the present house in 1767-80 as a showcase for the antique sculpture collected by William Weddell on his Grand Tour of Italy. The Hall's 18th-c. interiors by Adam are considered to be among the finest in Europe.

The house stands in 25 acres of gardens on the NE bank of the River Ure. The most famous set-pieces are the *Sculpture Galleries*, and the *Tapestry Room* with Gobelin tapestries; sculptures and tapestries form part of the overall Adam design which includes fine furniture and decoration by master-craftsmen such as Antonio Zucchi and Thomas Chippendale.

The *Grounds* contain rare shrubs and trees, and a series of formal gardens, each designed to show plants at their best for every season of the year. A miniature railway runs for over 1m along the riverside and through the gardens. There is an adventure garden for children.

Close to the entrance of the Hall is the Victorian **Church of Christ the Consoler** built by William Burges for Lady Mary Vyner in memory of her son, killed by Greek brigands. There is excellent stained glass designed by F. Weeks, a fine rose window and a jewelled altar frontal made by Lady Mary.

## Newton Dale                                      C2
*Dale off A169, N of Pickering*

Created about 10,000 years ago by glacial meltwaters, Newton Dale is a spectacular gorge cutting N-S through the E *North Yorkshire Moors* from Fen Bog (S of Goathland) to Pickering, often reaching a depth of several hundred feet. The dale was part of the Norman hunting forest of Pickering; from the 12th-14th c. iron was worked on the E edge. Today conifers line the W edge in the forest area that is part of Cropton Forest, owned by the Forestry Commission. Before the forest was planted in the 1920s the dale was farmed, and in the 19th c. the track for a railway from Pickering to Whitby was laid along the boggy floor of the dale. This is now preserved by the North

73

York Moors Historical Railway Trust, which owns 18m of track between Pickering and Grosmont in Esk Dale.

There are good forest walks centred on the *North Yorkshire Railway* stop, *Newtondale Halt.*

## Nidderdale B3

*N Yorks. Dale to SE of Yorkshire Dales National Park*

This is the smallest of Yorkshire's main western dales, the Nidd having a length of 50m and a drainage area of 212 sq m. The river rises just outside the boundary of the Yorkshire Dales National Park on the slopes of Great Whernside, which with Little Whernside flanks Coverdale. The Nidd flows SE through remote uplands to *Pateley Bridge*, the sightseeing, hiking and potholing centre of the upper dale. Entering mid-dale it flows past *Knaresborough*, where it cuts a gorge in the narrow belt of magnesian limestone which edges the fertile Plain of York. In its lower reaches the river crosses the plain to the pretty village of *Nun Monkton*, where it joins the Ouse.

The limestone country around Nidderdale rivals the *Craven* area further W for gorges, waterfalls and caverns. Natural phenomena like *Stump Cross Caverns* near Pateley Bridge and *How Stean Gorge* near *Lofthouse* are popular attractions, in the summer season, as are *Brimham Rocks*, also near Pateley Bridge.

In its upper reaches the dale is the traditional domain of shepherds, and more recently of waterwork employees tending the reservoirs that supply Bradford. Pot-holes abound in this remote area, and near Lofthouse the river actually disappears for 2m. Gradually the scene down-river becomes pastoral, until at the end of its course the Nidd is flowing through rich farmland.

## Northallerton B2

*N Yorks. Town on A167/A168/A684, 9m NW of Thirsk. EC Thur MD Wed, Sat*

Administrative centre for the county of North Yorkshire, Northallerton's position on the Boroughbridge-Durham turnpike road in the 18th and 19th c. endowed it with some fine coaching inns: *The Fleece Inn* is partly medieval, *The Golden Lion* graced with Doric columns. Halfway along High Street, the road widens to the market place; at the N end of the street, standing on a green among trees, is *All Saints' Church* with a Perpendicular pinnacled tower. The W doorway dates from *c.* 1200, the N arcade is of 1150, and the church has many fragments of Anglo-Saxon and Anglo-Danish carving.

Described as 'waste' in the Domesday Book and burned by Robert Bruce in 1318, Northallerton was long the county town of the North Riding. It is still one of North Yorkshire's liveliest commercial centres, its weekly livestock market busy with shoppers and traders from a wide area over this part of the York plain and the Vale of Mowbray.

3m N of the town is the site where the English defeated the Scots at the Battle of the Standard (1138).

**North York Moors National Park** see *North Yorkshire Moors*

## North Yorkshire Forests

*N Yorks*

The thick forests covering primitive England were seriously diminished when hunting tribes were superseded by cultivators and herdsmen. In what is now the North York Moors National Park, areas like the great hunting forest of Pickering survived as part of the Norman culture, but the woodlands steadily declined until the 18th and 19th c. when systematic planting was carried out by landowners who primarily wanted hunting cover and landscaped parks.

The Forestry Commission was established (1919) in response to depletion of the country's timber resources during World War I, and its earliest planting in the North Yorkshire Moors was carried out in 1923 around *Thornton Dale*. The FC now administers about 56,600 acres in North Yorkshire, of which 85% are forested, and there are also privately owned woodlands. The FC trees are mostly conifers which do well on moorland soil, but the soils of the Howardian Hills accept broadleafed trees as well as a wider range of conifers. Besides yielding timber, these properties have numerous picnic areas and waymarked forest trails, as well as other recreational facilities. Some of the best known features are described in Gazetteer entries under names of major forest areas designated by the FC; these names are not always shown on maps.

FC forest areas on the E side of the National Park are **Wykeham Forest** near *Scarborough*, **Dalby Forest** N of *Thornton Dale* village and **Cropton Forest** N of *Pickering*. On the W of the region are **Hambleton Forest**, centred on *Helmsley*, and **Cleveland Forest** in the *Cleveland Hills* around Osmotherley and overlooking Teesside.

## North Yorkshire Moors
*N Yorks*

Almost all this high plateau (1400ft at its highest point) contains the North York Moors National Park. Its natural boundaries are defined on the SW by the steep-sided Hambleton Hills rising from the Vale of Mowbray, on the NW and N by the Cleveland Hills which curve round to overlook Teesside, on the E by the North Sea cliffs and on the S by the flat shelf called the Tabular Hills, bordering the Vale of Pickering.

The moor's N and S edges are cleft by dales running down from the high land to the long, deep valley of *Esk Dale* (N) and to the Vale of Pickering (S). The River Esk runs E from below its source on *Westerdale Moor* and the dale opens out as it nears the North Sea where the old fishing town of *Whitby*, with its ruined clifftop abbey, forms the NE cornerstone of the National Park. Other cornerstones are at the seaside resort of *Scarborough* (SE), and at the market towns of *Thirsk* (SW) and *Guisborough* (NW). The Park's headquarters are at *Helmsley*, 14m E of Thirsk.

The **North York Moors National Park** which lies within these boundaries was designated in 1952 and covers 553 sq m of varied and dramatic scenery in what was once the North Riding. The heather and bracken-covered moors covering the heart of the plateau are weathered into distinctive 'riggs' between the deep incisions of the dales. They are criss-crossed by wayfarers' tracks and waymarked with cairns or with stone crosses like the well-known *Ralph Cross* which stands at the head of Rosedale, on Westerdale Moor.(See also *Castleton*.) These were used by monks from the great land-owning medieval abbeys set in the shelter of the dales, and by ironstone miners, jet traders, smugglers and funeral processions from isolated settlements to far-flung parish churches. Today the cross's image is used as the symbol for the National Park.

Some of the old tracks are followed by the long-distance walks, the *Cleveland Way* and the *Lyke Wake Walk*, which along their routes encounter wild coastal cliffs and forested areas as well as bleak moorland. The Forestry Commission lands cover 56,600 acres around the edge of the moors and some of the dales, most notably Newton Dale, through which the *North York Moors Railway* follows 18m of historical track from Pickering to Esk Dale.

The track passes some interesting sites in the Park, especially around *Goathland* with its waterfalls; near here, within walking distance of the line, is a well preserved stretch of Roman road, an ancient burial mound (Lilla Howe) and the futuristic radomes of the Early Warning Station of Fylingdales Moor. Historic buildings that can be visited include the dale abbeys of *Rievaulx* and *Byland*, as well as *Whitby Abbey*, Mount Grace Priory at *Osmotherley* and *Guisborough Priory*. Other villages and towns tell the history of the moors in their churches and museums.

(See also *North Yorkshire Forests*.)

## North Yorkshire Moors Railway  C2
*N Yorks. Historic railway route. Inf: Tel (0751) 72508*

Constructed by George Stephenson in 1836 to link Pickering and Whitby, the line is one of the oldest in the country. It was closed under the Beeching Plan in 1965, but was purchased by a band of enthusiasts who worked tirelessly to re-establish it, and was re-opened by the Duchess of Kent on May 1 1973. It is managed by the North York Moors Historical Railway Trust based at *Pickering* Station, where there is an Information Centre, an excellent bookshop and a restaurant.

The track covers 18m in the North York Moors National Park, running N from Pickering to Grosmont in *Esk Dale*, where it links with British Rail's Middlesbrough-Whitby line. From Pickering, the first of the three stations between the termini is near *Levisham*; 1½m from the village, the station is situated in the deep gorge of *Newton Dale*. The boggy dale floor, it is said, was fortified with brushwood and bales of wool before the track could be laid.

At *Newtondale Halt* the Forestry Commission has provided waymarked trails and picnic areas in Cropton Forest. The line from here climbs to its highest point (550ft) at *Eller Beck* before starting the descent to *Goathland* Station, where there are refreshment facilities and a gift shop. The line descends by way of the Eller Beck and the Murk Esk valleys, passing some spectacular examples of railway engineering.

Steam locomotives are the main attraction for railway enthusiasts and these are regularly used, supplemented by diesel engines. Daily time-tabled services are scheduled during the tourist season, bar facilities are available on most trains and on Wednesday-evening services between Pickering and Goathland a Pullman dining car is connected to the train. At *Grosmont* there is a large *engine shed* full of old steam locomotives, and a shed with a *viewing platform* where visitors can watch enthusiasts renovating and repairing rolling stock, some of which is also on view in the sidings. A gift shop and refreshments are also available.

## Nun Monkton                                      C3
*Nidderdale. Village off A59, 11m NW of York*

It is here that the Nidd flows into the Ouse, losing its identity while winding through a village of great beauty and style: a maypole stands on a large green with two duck ponds, surrounded by pleasant brick houses and cottages; an avenue leads to the Hall, which stands on the site of a Benedictine nunnery, and the church. An old weeping beech tree partly obscures the church.

Nun Monkton has a religious background dating from the mid-12th c., when the nunnery was founded on the site where the handsome, late 17th-c. brick-built *Hall* now stands. After the suppression of the nunnery, the village was granted to John Neville, Lord Latimer, whom Catherine Parr (the future, and last wife of Henry VIII) took as her second husband.

The nunnery chapel forms the aisleless nave of **St Mary's Church**, one of the most beautiful and unusual in Yorkshire, a combination of Norman, Transitional and Early English periods. Particularly noteworthy are the W front and its fine sculptures, the arcaded gallery of high lancet windows in the upper nave and some superb William Morris glass decorating three lancet windows in the E wall, which was restored in 1873.

## Nunnington Hall (NT)                             C2
*Ryedale. Historic house off B1257, 5m SE of Helmsley*

This fine part-Tudor manor house stands in peaceful gardens on the banks of the Rye, close to the 17th-c. triple-arched bridge. The estate was acquired by Richard Graham, later created Viscount Preston by Charles II, and it is he who was responsible for the manor's late 17th-c. work. His fine tomb (1695) can be seen in the village church, *All Saints and St James*.

The Hall's principal rooms include the panelled *Hall* with its handsome carved chimney-piece; one of the panelled bedrooms is supposed to be haunted. There are fine tapestries and china, and a magnificent 19th-c. *dolls' house*. A special gallery houses the Carlisle Collection of miniature rooms furnished in different periods. On the river's banks is a haunted wood, and peacocks strut across the lawns.

## Osmotherley                                      B2
*N Yorks. Village off A19, 6m NE of Northallerton*

This village, beautifully situated in a cleft of the Cleveland Hills, is at the W end of the *Lyke Wake Walk* and is a turning-point on the *Cleveland Way*. The stone cottages with pantiled roofs have as a centre of attraction a *Market Hall*; on a small green is an ancient *market cross*, and a *stone table* which was probably well used when markets featured regularly in village life. John Wesley preached at this table, and down a narrow passage close to the green is one of England's earliest *Methodist Chapels* with the date 1754 over the doorway. *St Peter's Church*, SW of the green, has evidence of Anglo-Saxon origins and a Norman S doorway, but was much restored in 1892.

1m N near the junction of the A172 and the A19 at *The Cleveland Tontine Inn* stands the ruin of **Mount Grace Priory** (NT), founded in 1398. It is sheltered under the moors beneath dense hanging woods, and is favoured with a magnificent display of daffodils in the spring. The best preserved of Britain's nine Carthusian monasteries, it retains substantial parts of its church, courts, cells and gatehouse; around the great cloister can be seen doorways and food hatches for the monks who lived in strict seclusion. One of the individual cells has been restored, and there is much to show the monks' way of life in the layout of their single cells and walled greens.

Just outside the gatehouse stands the priory *Guest House*, converted in 1654 into a private dwelling. On the hilltop above the priory is the 16th-c. *Lady Catherine Chapel*, once a pilgrims' shrine; after the Dissolution it was granted to the last prior, and his dwelling can also be seen. There is a fine view across the Plain of York.

## Otley                                            B3
*Wharfedale. Pop 13,826. On A659/A660/A6038/B6451, 6m E of Ilkley. EC Wed MD Fri. Inf: Tel (0943) 465151*

Otley nestles at the foot of the 900ft-high **Chevin**, a tree-covered moorland escarpment which for centuries has been the site of beacon fires lit at times of national rejoicing. An ancient seven-arched bridge straddles the River Wharfe to connect both sides of this pleasant old market and manufacturing town. N of the river the town is modern and residential, while the S side has the older commercial and industrial centre with a maypole and *Butter Cross*. A Victorian *Golden Jubilee Clock* bears a tablet of gratitude given by Belgian refugees who received hospitality here during World War I.

**All Saints' Church**, founded in the 7th c., is mainly of 14th and 15th c. construction but retains some Norman work and has a Georgian S porch. Of main interest is a collection of Anglo-Saxon sculpture: fragments of crosses with rich carvings of people and animals. The church holds memorials to the Fairfax and Fawkes families, respectively of *Denton Hall* near *Ilkley* and *Farnley Hall*, 2m N of Otley. In the churchyard is a *monument* commemorating over 30 men killed during the construction of Bramhope Tunnel on the line between Harrogate and Leeds; it is a stone scale-model of the tunnel mouth.

Otley is the birthplace of Thomas Chippendale, whose baptism on June 5, 1718 is recorded in the parish registers; the site of his birthplace is marked by a *plaque*. Examples of this great craftsman's work can be seen at *Harewood House*, at *Newby Hall* and in other great houses in Yorkshire and throughout Britain.

The **Museum** is in the Civic Centre, Cross Green and has an interesting collection of local history exhibits. The moorland S has evidence of prehistoric hut circles and cairns.

2m N on the B6451 is the Tudor *Farnley Hall*, overlooking the Wharfe. It was visited on several occasions by J.M.W. Turner, who was inspired by the changing scene outside; the house contains a fine collection of his works. Another guest may have been Guy Fawkes, visiting relatives; the house has always belonged to the Fawkes family. The house is closed to the public.

### Pateley Bridge
B3
*Nidderdale. Town on B6265, 14m NW of Harrogate. EC Thur. Inf: Tel (0423) 711147*

A market town in medieval times, picturesque Pateley Bridge stands partly on the valley bottom and partly on a steep hillside flanking the River Nidd's E bank. The town is a good base from which to explore the higher reaches of Nidderdale and the surrounding moors; the limestone country here produces unusual rock formations, pot-holes and caves.

Between Pateley Bridge and the village of Wath, on the minor road leading up-dale to *Ramsgill*, is the old Foster Beck water-powered *Hemp Mill*: now a restaurant, the building retains its water wheel. Just at the edge of town on this road, opposite *St Cuthbert's Church* (1827), the **Nidderdale Museum** has a good collection of Dales' bygones. High on the S of town the old church, *St Mary's*, stands in ruins at the top of Old Church Lane, looking across to the

moors. St Mary's can be reached, *via* a flight of steps and *Panorama Walk*, from the top of High Street.

Across the river the B6265 ascends Greenhow Hill, and passes *Stump Cross Caverns*; to the SE of the town, off the same road, are the fantastic *Brimham Rocks*. Closer to the town is the rugged gorge known as *Ravensgill*, with a lake and woodlands, reached by an energetic trek from the village of *Bewerley*. On the S side of the village a road rises steeply to the summit of *Guy's Cliff*, on which is perched **Yorke's Folly**; like many of its kind, this mock ruin was built to provide work in lean times.

### Pennine Way
A1/A2
*N Yorks. Long-distance footpath*

The first of Britain's long-distance paths, the Pennine Way was opened on April 23, 1965. 250m long, it runs from Derbyshire's Peak District to the Cheviot Hills, only a short stretch passing through the Dales.

From the S the Way enters the Yorkshire Dales National Park at Gargrave near Skipton to encounter some of the striking and characteristic limestone landscape of the *Craven* district by following the course of the River Aire through *Malham* and then skirting Pen-y-Ghent near *Settle*. It climbs out of Ribblesdale and past the head of Wharfedale where it joins the *Dalesway* for a short distance.

The Way passes *Hawes* near the famous *Hardrow Force* in Wensleydale, then makes a great loop W of *Buttertubs Pass* to Swaledale, passes *Thwaite* and crosses the dale to *Keld*, where it climbs due N to Durham and *The Tan Hill Inn*.

### Pickering
C2
*Ryedale. Town on A169/A170, 8m N of Malton. Events: Carnival (1st or 2nd week in Jul); Traction Engine Rally (last week in Jul). EC Wed MD Mon. Inf: Tel (0751) 73791*

'Gateway to the Moors', Pickering stands on the beck of the same name at the N edge of the Vale of Pickering, about halfway between Helmsley and Scarborough, with the moors spreading N. The town centres on its long, sloping market place which descends from church to the railway station. One of the oldest parts of Pickering, it is bustling and congested on market days. There are many narrow, attractive streets with red-roofed cottages, houses, inns and shops jumbled together, their grey stones brightened in spring by thousands of crocuses and daffodils which bloom along the roadsides.

On the hill N of the market place are the ruins of the **Castle**, built between 1180 and the early 14th c. It seems to have held a special attraction for royalty, since it is known that at least eight monarchs stayed there, and possibly a ninth – Richard II, as a prisoner. A fair amount remains: the motte, sections of curtain walling and five towers; the restored *Chapel* and (the oldest part of the castle) the original *Hall*.

The 14th-c. spire of the **Church of St Peter and St Paul** is a landmark seen from miles across the Vale. Much restored in the 19th c., the church's building progress can be followed from early Norman times through the medieval period to the 15th c; this is the date of the remarkable **murals** for which the Church is famed. The extensive range of paintings, among the finest in the country, was discovered under layers of whitewash in 1853, and hastily re-covered. 25 years later a more enlightened vicar revealed them: crude and vivid representations of lives of the saints, and biblical scenes, including Herod's Feast, St George and the Dragon, the Martyrdom of St Edmund and the Murder of Thomas à Becket. The church also has some interesting *memorials*, among them those of Robert and Nicholas King (who surveyed Washington DC in 1812), and John and William Marshall the pioneer agriculturists, who opened England's first agricultural college (1818) at their home in the present **Beck Isle Museum of Rural Life** in leafy Potter Hill. They also initiated the idea for what is now the Ministry of Agriculture and Fisheries. In their 18th-c. house *Beck Hall*, which stands by Pickering's restored medieval *bridge*, the museum houses a fine display illustrating the domestic and working life of the town and surrounding district.

A connection with a museum on a grander scale is the association of *Houndgate Hall*, in Hungate, with the famous Castle Museum in York: the Hall was the former home of Dr J.L. Kirk. A noted antiquary, he amassed an enormous collection of local artefacts and bygones which he gave to the City of *York*. The Hall has more recently served as the first 'Skeldale House' in films based on James Herriot's books. The stars and production team of *All Creatures Great and Small* had their headquarters next door at *The Forest and Vale Hotel*, built as a mansion late in the 18th c. (See also *Herriot Country*.)

The hotel is well named, since Pickering stands at the foot of *Newton Dale*, which has the Cropton Forest along its W edge. The *North Yorkshire Moors Railway* runs through the dale from Pickering to Grosmont in Esk Dale, following an 18m historical route, and the Forestry Commission has

waymarked walks and picnic areas near the second stop from here, *Newtondale Halt*. An Information Centre at *Pickering Station* gives time-tables and details about interesting features on the route, and also has information about forest beauty spots in this part of the *North Yorkshire Forests*.

3m S of Pickering *Kirby Misperton Hall*, which was the home of George IV's chaplain, now serves as the centre of a leisure park known as **Flamingoland**. The Hall was a gift from the king, and by way of thanks his chaplain erected an *obelisk* nearby. The park's amusements include a fairground, a monorail, model and miniature railways, and a working farm. A camping holiday village has been set up and the village's entertainments rooms now occupy the old Hall.

**Plompton Rocks** see *Harrogate*

**Ramsgill**                                                      B3
*Nidderdale. Village off B6265, 5m NW of Pateley Bridge*

Ramsgill is a pretty little place with a green and pleasant cottages, and an attractive hotel. It is situated on the River Nidd at the N end of *Gouthwaite Reservoir*, a favourite resort of ornithologists attracted by large numbers of geese, waterfowl and waders which between them provide interest the year round.

The village was the birthplace of Eugene Aram, the local schoolmaster and self-taught scholar who was to end his life on the gallows after being convicted of murder at *Knaresborough* (1759). His story has been immortalised by Lord Lytton in his book *Eugene Aram*, and by Thomas Hood's ballad of the same title.

From Ramsgill the road takes a pretty riverside route past Lofthouse to the high reaches of Nidderdale, and *How Stean Gorge* (see *Lofthouse*).

**Ravenscar**                                                   D2
*N Yorks. Village off A171, 15m NW of Scarborough. Nat Trust Inf: Tel (0723) 870138*

The most pleasant part of Ravenscar is away from the village on the cliff top around *The Raven Hall Hotel*, which occupies part of an 18th-c. house and stands on a Roman signal station. The headland is some 600ft above sea level and commands extensive views N to Robin Hood's Bay.

A pathway to the shore leads past the golf course of the hotel, the grounds of which are open to non-residents for a nominal charge. The pleasant gardens end at castellated stone walls forming terraces on the cliff edge, and there is an open-air swimming pool also available to non-residents. Close to the hotel entrance is a National Trust shop and *Information Centre* with geological and other displays, and information about the locality. One exhibit explains the attempt to create an elegant resort here in the 18th c.

Ravenscar is on the route of the *Cleveland Way* (see *Walk 6*, p. 24), and is the E end of the *Lyke Wake Walk*.

### Reeth                                                  A2
*Swaledale. Village on B6270, 10m W of Richmond. Inf: Tel (0748) 84373*

Reeth is situated on Arkle Beck, where Arkengarthdale (N) joins Swaledale. It was once a market town serving the surrounding farming and mining communities, but lead mining has long since ceased and the new industry is tourism. The change is reflected in the abandoned mining relics scattered over Arkengarthdale fells and in the cafés, hotels and shops clustered around Reeth's extensive green in company with the fine stone houses of a bygone age.

Reeth stands at the edge of '*Herriot Country*', and figures in the author's descriptions of life as a Dales vet; the **Swaledale Folk Museum** also reflects the lives of Dales sheep farmers and lead miners in interesting exhibits on such subjects as local housing and schooling, Poor Laws, public houses and Methodism. The local agricultural show which is held here every August is a typical Dales event, and featured in the television serial *All Creatures Great and Small*.

A quiet road from Reeth reaches **Marrick Priory**, a ruined 12th-c. Benedictine nunnery standing in woodland on the N bank of the Swale, where the water rushes over a rocky bed. This peaceful place is also approached from *Marrick* village (1m E) down the *Nuns' Causey*: moss-covered stone steps beneath the trees. Beautifully situated across the water, lower down the dale, are the ruins of **Ellerton Priory**, a 15th-c. Cistercian nunnery consisting of a tower and the remains of a church.

### Ribblesdale                                            A3
*N Yorks. Dale in Yorkshire Dales National Park*

The River Ribble in Craven rises near the source of the Wharfe, and flows S to *Settle* on the S border of the National Park. Followed from here by the route of the A65, it continues S to enter Lancashire at the E edge of the Bowland Forest.

The chief features of interest in Ribblesdale are the famous 'three peaks': the highest point in North Yorkshire, *Whernside* (2414ft), *Ingleborough* on the W of the dale,

and *Pen-y-Ghent* on the E. These long smooth-topped hills are familiar landmarks in all parts of *Craven*. This is limestone country at its most striking: pot-holes and waterfalls abound, and the area is a walkers' and cavers' paradise. (See also *Ingleton*.)

The *Pennine Way* skirts Pen-y-Ghent on its route N from Malhamdale; after descending to the quarrying village of Horton-in-Ribblesdale the Way leads to Ribblehead, then continues to *Hawes* in Wensleydale.

### Richmond                                               B2
*N Yorks. Town on A6108/A6136 B6271/B6274, 11m NE of Leyburn. EC Wed MD Sat. Inf: Tel (0748) 3525 (summer) (0748) 4221 (winter)*

This old town of cobbled streets and narrow wynds grew around its castle, situated on a crag above the river. The spacious, sloping *Market Place*, surrounded with Georgian and Victorian buildings, is the focal point from which all else radiates. A huge *obelisk* erected here in 1771 as a replacement for the old market cross commemorates the 700th anniversary of the founding of the castle. Another eye-catching structure in the square is the redundant *Holy Trinity Church*, founded *c.* 1135. Unusual, if not unique, is its tower separated from the rest of the church by a building now used as offices; from it are rung the 'Prentice Bell at 8am and the Curfew Bell at 8pm, and on Shrove Tuesdays the Pancake Bell at 11am. In its time the church has served as an assize court, prison, school, warehouse and granary; it is now the **Regimental Museum of the Green Howards**. Some interesting collections of local history can also be seen in the **Richmondshire Museum** in Ryder's Wynd.

NE of the market place is a garden in which stands *Greyfriars Tower*, all that remains of a church founded in 1288 but never completed. The 15th-c. tower is pierced by a graceful arch, and the buttresses reach up to pinnacled battlements. Between here and the market place, in Friars' Wynd, is the Georgian **Theatre Royal**, an unpretentious building from the outside, but inside one of tremendous character and delight; a unique treasure of Georgian England still in use today. This tiny theatre was opened in 1788 by an actor-manager named Samuel Butler, and its decline came in 1830 with the ending of the Butler family tradition. In 1848 the pit was boarded over, and during a long period of obscurity the building was used variously as wine vaults, an auction room, a corn chandler's store, a furniture store and, during World War II, a salvage depot.

Restoration began with the foundation of a Trust in 1960; reopening was in 1963, and the theatre has opened for every holiday season since. In the boxes, each named after a famous playwright, the green upholstered seats give way to gilt-painted basket chairs. The gallery and pit are stepped to give a perfect view of the stage. Guided tours take place at regular intervals throughout the season, and visitors may wander around the **Museum** with its collection of memorabilia, including Britain's oldest complete set of painted scenery (1836).

Richmond's most prominent landmark is the great **Castle** begun in 1071. Its turreted, battlemented keep, 109ft high and with walls 11ft thick, was built over the original gatehouse in 1146. Two towers in the curtain wall survive, and the Great Hall, or *Scolland's Hall*. Built in 1080, it is said to be the oldest hall in England. From the keep there is a grand view of town, moors and river.

The river is crossed by two bridges which have, conversely, fine views of the castle. The upstream *bridge* is a narrow stone buttressed structure designed by the York architect John Carr in 1789; from here the river flows swiftly and turbulently around the castle crag before passing beneath the modern bridge. Near the old bridge is the green, and from here can be seen the *Culloden Tower*, a folly constructed by a local MP as a memorial to the famous battle of 1746. Restored as a holiday home by the Landmark Trust, its interior was designed in a variety of styles.

Close to the new bridge, overlooking the Swale, is **St Mary's Church**, a Victorian building on a 12th-c. foundation. Some early 16th-c. stalls from *\*Easby Abbey* have intriguing misericords, the most humorous being that of a pig playing the bagpipes, with piglets dancing to the tune. In the chancel is a monument to Sir Thomas Hutton (d. 1629), showing husband and wife and their dozen children; the *Green Howards' Memorial Chapel* has banners connected with the Regiment's history, and furnishings by the modern wood carver, Robert Thompson of *\*Kilburn*. In the churchyard is a *Plague Stone*, a memorial to over 1000 people who succumbed to plague in the 17th c., and also the grave of William Willance who, on a foggy night in 1606, miraculously escaped when he and his horse plunged over *Whitecliffe Scar*, 2½m W on Beacon Hill, between Richmond and Marske. An *obelisk* marks the spot, since known as Willance's Leap. (See *Walk 3*, p. 23.)

Of Richmond's celebrities easily the best known is Frances I'Anson who lived at '*Hill House*' which still stands near Greyfriars' Tower off the Darlington Road. Frances is better known as the 'Lass of Richmond Hill' after the song written by her husband, Leonard McNally, whom she married in 1787. The following year she was present at the opening of the theatre: at its re-opening 175 years later the song was sung in her honour and memory.

Although far from the sea, Richmond has at least two maritime connections. Henry Greathead was born here, and at South Shields in 1790 a lifeboat that he built was the first ever to go into service. 3m N of Richmond, *Hartforth Hall* was the birthplace of Rear-Admiral Sir Christopher Cradock, Commander of the fleet which engaged a German force at the Battle of Coronel on November 1, 1914. Cradock went down with the *Good Hope*, and there are memorials to him in York Minster and in St Agatha's Church at Gilling West.

5m E of Richmond, *Moulton Hall* (NT), rebuilt in the late 17th c., can be visited by arrangement with the tenant.

3m S of the town is the village of *Hipswell*, believed to be the birthplace of the 14th-c. reformer John Wyclif.

### Rievaulx Abbey        C2

*Ryedale. Off B1257, 3m NW of Helmsley*

Yorkshire's first Cistercian abbey (1131), Rievaulx was founded in a steep, wooded valley so narrow that the usual E-W orientation had to be ignored. Standing close to the River Rye, its substantial and romantic ruins give a good idea of what the establishment must have looked like in its 12th-c. heyday. With Fountains Abbey they represent England's finest abbey remains.

The roofless 12th-c. *nave* has finely proportioned arches and arcading, while the *choir* is a fine example of 13th-c. Early English architecture. The *Monastic Buildings* include, to the S of the cloister, the kitchen, refectory and warming house; to the E the chapter house, tunnel-vaulted vestry, meeting room and undercroft with dormitory above; and on the W side the lay brothers' accommodation. There was a separate infirmary block and cloister to the E of the main range of buildings which later became the abbot's lodgings.

Overlooking the valley from the S and E is *\*Rievaulx Terrace*, laid out in the mid-18th c. to give the finest view of the abbey ruins. The abbey and terrace lie close to the *\*Cleveland Way*, and the forest area has waymarked walks and picnic sites (see *Walk 4*, p. 23).

**Rievaulx Terrace and Temples** (NT)  C2
*Ryedale. On B1257, 2m NW of Helmsley*

Laid out by Thomas Duncombe III *c.* 1758 as part of *Duncombe Park*, the curved, grassy terrace and adjoining woodland are beautifully situated on an escarpment overlooking the ruined \*Rievaulx Abbey and across the Rye Valley to the Hambleton Hills. At the terrace's N end is a rectangular Ionic Temple, and ½m S is a smaller, round temple of the Tuscan order. From the terrace there is a splendid view of the abbey below.

The magnificent interior of the *Ionic Temple* is dominated by the splendid *fresco* of mythological scenes on the ceiling and gone by the Italian artist Giuseppe Borgnis. The carved woodwork of the frieze, overmantle and door casing, and the white marble chimney-piece, are also noteworthy. The fine pieces of furniture include a set of 18th-c. mahogany dining chairs. Two food-preparation rooms in the basement display Victorian photographs from the Duncombe family albums and an *Exhibition* devoted to the Rievaulx Terrace and Temples.

The *Tuscan Temple* has a dome made up of bands of guilloches and rosettes with a painted roundel in the centre of a winged female deity. The floor is covered with a 13th-c. tesselated pavement reputed to have been discovered near the high altar of the abbey in 1821.

The Helmsley-Stokesley road passing close to Rievaulx Terrace continues N through \*Bilsdale, where there are good views and picnic areas.

**Ripley**  B3
*Nidderdale. Village off A61/B6165, 4m N of Harrogate*

Ripley has a distinctly French appearance which can be traced to 1827 when the local squire, Sir William Amcotts Ingilby, remodelled it as a typical Alsace Lorraine village, apparently for no other reason than that he happened to like the style: he even labelled the Village Hall the *Hotel de Ville*. Once a market town, this is a neat and pretty place with a single wide, tree-shaded street bordered by broad grass verges and delightful stone cottages; in the cobbled market square are the market cross and stocks.

Tucked away in trees behind the cottages is the battlemented Tudor **Castle**, the original tower adjoined to a house rebuilt in 1780. It stands in pleasant gardens and parkland with lakes fed by Thornton Beck, and is entered through a massive 15th-c. *Gatehouse* opening onto a courtyard. Over the archway is the inscription: *Parlez au Suisse*. The castle has been the home of the

Ingilby family for over six centuries. In the Tudor part is a floor made from the deck of a British Man-o'-War, a priest's hole and a good display of Civil War armour and weaponry: James I and Cromwell both stayed here, Cromwell uninvited. By contrast the 18th-c. section has elegant mantlepieces, chandeliers, furniture and pictures. The *Grounds* were laid out by 'Capability' Brown, and are planted with specimen trees from many parts of the world.

Just S, near a bridge crossing the beck, the 15th-c. **All Saints' Church** bears tragic reminders of the Civil War: indentations in the stonework of the E wall were caused by musket-balls from Cromwell's firing squads as they executed Royalist villagers who had fought at Marston Moor. The church has a priest's room over the *S Chapel*. There are several memorials and tombs of the Ingilby family, including a black taffeta tabard decorated with a coat of arms, part of the paraphernalia of funerals in days long ago. In the churchyard is an unusual object, an ancient *'kneeling'* or *'weeping'* cross with eight niches in the stone to receive the knees of penitents. It is thought to be the only one of its kind in the country.

**Ripon**  B3
*N Yorks. Pop 12,580. 11m N of Harrogate on A61/A6108/B6265. Event: Feast of St Wilfrid (Aug). EC Wed MD Thur. Inf: Tel (0765) 4625*

Standing at the confluence of the Rivers Ure, Skell and Laver, Ripon began as a community which grew up around a timber monastery founded in 657. This was followed in 672 by the nucleus of the present cathedral, commenced by St Wilfrid, whose authority was bestowed on him by the Synod of Whitby in 664. Following the destruction of the early church in 960, rebuilding was carried out after the Norman Conquest; St Wilfrid's original crypt now lies at the heart of the present building.

**Cathedral of St Peter and St Wilfrid** The present structure is largely the work of Archbishop Roger of York (1154-81). The splendid *W front*, with its lancet windows, was remodelled over successive centuries and presents a mixture of architectural styles; this mixture is seen again in the central tower which was partly rebuilt in the 15th c. and combines Early English and Perpendicular. Inside, the *nave* is also a rebuilding: originally aisleless, its aisles were added in the 16th c. The fine 12th-c. *chancel* is Archbishop Roger's work, while the timber vault belongs to Sir George Gilbert Scott's remodelling of 1862, in which he retained the 14th-c. bosses showing a series of biblical scenes. An outstandingly attractive feature of the 15th-c. stalls is the carving of the misericords, featuring the vigorous and eloquent craftsmanship of the noted 'Ripon Carvers' and depicting various amusing creatures and scenes. *St Wilfrid's Crypt* holds the cathedral's treasury, displaying plate from all parts of the diocese.

The diocese of Ripon was created in 1836, and embraces the City of Leeds as well as local rural communities. The market place is dominated by a 90ft *obelisk*, erected in 1780 to commemorate William Aislabie's 60 years as local Member of Parliament. During this time, Aislabie acquired the ruin of *\*Fountains Abbey* and incorporated it into the gracefully landscaped park at *Studley Royal*. His commemorative obelisk – which may be said to serve as Ripon's market cross – also commemorates the city's 1000 year-old nightly ceremony of Blowing the Wakeman's Horn, since it is surmounted by the shape of a horn as weather vane.

The horn is blown at 9 o'clock each evening at the four corners of the market place and outside the Mayor's residence by the 'Wakeman' in a tricorn hat; the tradition dates from 886, when Alfred the Great granted a charter and the horn of a wild ox was presented to the city for the purpose of setting the watch. The ceremony has recently become a tourist attraction. The original horn is kept with the civic regalia in the *Town Hall*, designed by James Wyatt (1801). This handsome building in the market place displays large gilt letters which proclaim: 'Except ye Lord keep ye cittie, ye Wakeman waketh in vain'. The last proper Wakeman, or night watchman, was Hugh Ripley who became the first Mayor and lived in the 13th-c. *Wakeman's House*, a black and white timbered building in the SE corner of the market place. The building is used as an information centre, and houses the town's **Museum**. Another museum, which claims to be the first of its kind in Britain, is the **Ripon Prison and Police Museum** which can be visited in St Marygate.

Close to the cathedral is *St Agnes Lodge*, a late 15th-c. house where it is believed Mary, Queen of Scots stayed on her way from Bolton Castle to Tutbury.

**Norton Conyers**, a Jacobean manor house off the A61 4m N of Ripon, was visited by Charlotte Brontë in the 19th c.; she made it 'Thornfield Hall' in *Jane Eyre*. The house has an interesting collection of furniture and pictures, and a display of wedding dresses belonging to the Graham family which has lived here since 1624. The 18th-c. walled garden has a *Garden Centre*.

Another kind of garden can be visited at **Lightwater Valley Leisure Centre**, 3m NW of Ripon on the A6108: there are wide-ranging outdoor activities for adults and children. 1m NE of Ripon off the A61 in the village of *Sharow*, *St John's Churchyard* has a stone pyramid surmounted by a cross. This is the appropriately designed tomb of Charles Piazzi Smyth, an astronomer of some repute who measured the great Pyramid of Gizeh. The National Trust here cares for the remains of the only surviving *cross* to mark the limits of sanctuary attached to St Wilfrid's abbey.

3m S of Ripon on a minor road off the A61 near Fountains Abbey is **Markenfield Hall**, a fine example of an English manor house of the 14th-16th c. It has a moat across which a bridge leads to the gatehouse. The 30ft-long *Chapel* and the 40ft-long *Banqueting Hall* are on the first floor; a turreted staircase leading to the hall adds to the attraction of the house.

### Robin Hood's Bay D2

*N Yorks. Village on B1447, 6m SE of Whitby. EC Wed*

Popular with artists, the village is in two parts. That at the top of the hill provides accommodation and refreshment, a magnificent view across rooftops and over the bay to Ravenscar, and a car park. From here, a walk down the 1-in-3 hill leads to the sea.

In the lower part of the village, the old cottages and shops huddle closely together on the cliff face behind a new wall erected to hinder further encroachment of the sea, which in the last two centuries has claimed a number of dwellings. There are only two streets, little more than a car's width, for local traffic; for the rest, just pedestrian passageways which make the place even more attractive. Both streets end at a slipway giving access to a rocky shoreline, a geologists' paradise at low tide; S of the rocky area is a beach with safe bathing. The route of the long-distance walk, the *\*Cleveland Way*, passes along the clifftop.

The Bay gets its name from the legend that Robin Hood was chased here, and escaped the clutches of his enemies by disguising himself as a fisherman. It appears under the name of 'Bramblewick' in the first three novels of Leo Walmsley, who lived here from 1894-1913 and used this picturesque village as the setting for his books.

**Roppa Edge** see *Bilsdale*

**Roseberry Topping** see *Great Ayton*

**Rosedale** C2
*Ryedale. Dale NW of Pickering*
The little River Seven rises in the Cleveland Hills and flows through Rosedale on its way to join the River Rye at Little Habton in the Vale of Pickering. It helps relieve the starkness of the dale whose steep slopes, almost bare of trees, make for a harsher prospect than neighbouring Farndale (W). Of the three communities in the dale, by far the largest is *Rosedale Abbey*; *Up Dale* is N, and *Hartoft* S.

In the 19th c., the dale was alive with activity as miners struggled to wrest ironstone from the moorland ridge and transport it by horse-drawn wagon to the station at Pickering. The method was abandoned when the moorland railroad was built to convey the stone to the Cleveland ironworks. A flavour of those far-off days remains, because the abandoned workings can still be seen scattered about the landscape. The railway was a remarkable affair, running along the edge of the valley and around the head of Farndale, and reaching a height of 1300ft before descending by means of a rope-worked incline to Battersby. The old track is now part of the *Lyke Wake Walk* route.

The road out of the valley to Hutton-le-Hole is a 1-in-3 incline known as the 'Rosedale Chimney' after a structure chimney that used to form part of the mine workings near the top of the hill; it was demolished as recently as 1972. 1¼m NE of Dale Head Farm is *Loose Howe Barrow*, in which were discovered human remains and Bronze Age artefacts last century.

**Rudston** see *Burton Agnes*

**Runswick Bay** C1
*N Yorks. Village off A174, 9m NW of Whitby*
Beloved of artists and photographers, this delightful fishing village climbs the slopes of a steep cliff N of a deep, wide bay; it is unusual for its absence of roads. The cottages, many of them now holiday homes, huddle haphazardly over the cliff face, linked by steps and narrow walkways. Many have attractive gardens, and the whole scene is one of great charm. There is a sandy beach and safe bathing. The modern village is at the top of the cliff, and is passed by the route of the *Cleveland Way* long-distance walk.

**Sandsend** C1
*N Yorks. Village on A174, 3m NW of Whitby*
This village is aptly named, since the Whitby sands end here, giving way to cliff scenery which shows considerable evidence of the alum workings of last century. The best part of the village is at the N end, where the road climbs steeply up *Lythe Bank*. Here a pretty valley cuts inland from the sea, and the old stone and tiled cottages with their attractive gardens are spread out on both banks of a small stream. Nearby are the **Mulgrave Woods**, part of the Mulgrave Castle estate of the Lord Lieutenant of North Yorkshire, the Marquess of Normandy.

There are pleasant walks in the area, one of which follows the route of the *Cleveland Way*.

**Scarborough** D2
*N Yorks. Pop 43,300. 20m SE of Whitby (A165/A64/A171/A171) Events: Scarborough International Festival (early Jun); International Motor Cycle Races and Cricket Festival (Sep); Carnival (2nd & 3rd weeks in Sep). EC Mon, Wed MD Thur. Inf: Tel (0723) 372261/373333*
The 'Queen of Watering Places', resort and conference centre, is situated on two large bays on either side of a high promontory on which stands the 12th-c. castle, with the splendid Marine Drive along the North Bay, and the old town clinging to the land at the N end of the South Bay.

The *Esplanade* is devoted to amusement arcades and seafood stalls; the harbour is large enough to contain the town's fishing fleet, pleasure boats and vessels from continental ports trading principally in timber. Adjoining the harbour is a sandy beach, which can largely disappear in the summer under an avalanche of visitors. Cliff lifts operate between the town and the shore, at the centre from St Nicholas Cliff, to the N from Alexandra Gardens and to the S from South Cliff. In Sandside (the street alongside the harbour) a café occupies *Richard III's House*; here also at No 9 is the 18th-c. *Customs House*. There are many interesting old buildings here, with Georgian and early Victorian houses to be seen in the streets climbing behind the harbour and to the W towards the modern commercial and shopping centre.

The South Bay shoreline running SE from the harbour has the delightful *Holbeck* and *Italian Gardens* and cliff walkways; down on the shore is a sea-water swimming pool and the *Spa* where daily light music summer concerts are given in a Palm Court atmosphere. High on the cliff near here is Scarborough's – and possibly England's – most grandiose hotel, *The Grand Hotel* by Cuthbert Broderick who designed Leeds Town Hall on a similar scale; it has a room for every day of the year. The **Crescent Art Gallery** and **Wood End Natural History Museum** in the elegant *Crescent* (1830-2), and the **Rotunda Archaeological Museum** in Vernon Road, are all situated close to the 70ft high *Valley Bridge*. *Wood End* is the former residence of the Sitwell family. The Victorian-Gothic **St Martin's Church** by G.F. Bodley in Albion Road is remarkable for Pre-Raphaelite work by Morris and Burne-Jones, Rossetti, Stanhope and Brown.

Inland from South Bay is *Oliver's Mount*, with panoramic views of coast and country; each year motor-cycle races are held in the winding lanes whose hairpin bends add to the hazards. Below and along the Mount's W flank is the *Mere* with a variety of waterfowl, where fishing, boating and canoeing are popular in summer, as well as woodland walks around the Mere.

The North Bay area is mainly residential, with numerous hotels and some boarding houses, and with *Alexandra* and *Northstead Manor Gardens*, and **Peasholme Park**. Between them they comprise extensive pleasure grounds including formal gardens, outdoor amusements, an open-air theatre, a stream and a boating lake with a collection of waterfowl. On the lake, in the holiday season, naval battles are fought using large-scale model warships. There are also water-sport facilities, a **Zoo and Marineland**, and a fairground. There is a chairlift from here to the sandy beach, which has plenty of rocky pools.

On the promontory, with magnificent views of both bays, the **Castle** stands on the site of a Roman signal station and of Bronze Age and Iron Age settlements. The castle dates from 1127 and is entered by the 13th-c. *Barbican*, opening on to the great *Keep* built from 1158-69. The round towers of the curtain walls date from the late 12th and early 13th c., and it was then that the original construction of **St Mary's Church**, just below the castle, took place. In the churchyard is the grave of Anne Brontë.

The town is well equipped to entertain the numerous visitors who arrive throughout the season on holidays or day trips. There are shops, cinemas, theatres and sporting facilities of all kinds, including the town's two golf courses and the championship course at *Ganton* 8m SW on the A64.

8m W on the A170 is the village of *Brompton*: here, in 1802, Wordsworth married Mary Hutchinson in *All Saints' Church*. In a small stone roadside building at the W end of the village, a *plaque* commemorates the life and work of the inventor Sir George Cayley. Among other achievements (such as inventing the first heavier than air machine in 1808), he

designed the *Sea Cut* so that the flood waters of the Derwent, a traditional threat to the rich flat farmlands of the *\*Vale of Pickering*, could drain E from near the top of Forge Valley through Scalby Beck to the North Sea.

From West Ayton on the A170 between Brompton and Scarborough, a minor road leads N through the beautiful, wooded *Forge Valley* down which the Derwent flows from Fylingdales Moor. The road continues N to *\*Hackness*.

The area inland from Scarborough is an interesting mixture of forested dales and heather moors, making the town a good base for varied excursions and walks. The *\*North Yorkshire Moors*, and the National Park, lie to the NW. The Forestry Commission's **Wykeham Forest**, to the W, has trails, viewpoints and picnic areas (see also *\*North Yorkshire Forests*). The *\*Cleveland Way* passes by on the last leg of its long trek S down the coast. Information about the walk and about the North York Moors National Park is available from the *Tourist Information Centre* in Harcourt Place, St Nicholas Cliff, which also provides further details on the fascinating history of England's first seaside resort.

### Scorton
B2

*N Yorks. Village on B1263, 6m E of Richmond*

The village surrounds an enormous walled green, and its old houses, *Grammar School (c. 1720)*, inns and shops make it an attractive place. It is best known for its archery competition: the Scorton Silver Arrow, the oldest sporting trophy in England, is competed for annually at a venue selected by the previous year's winner. The contest was first held in 1673.

### Sharow see *Ripon*

### Semerwater
A2

*Wensleydale. Lake off A684, 2m SW of Bainbridge*

Semerwater in its idyllic situation amid the hills is reached from the village of *\*Bainbridge* which stands S of the River Ure in upper Wensleydale. From the main dale highway small roads lead to either side of the lake, a relic of retreating Ice Age glaciers which blocked the valley mouth with debris. A further product of the Ice Age can be seen near where the roads descend to the northern shore: the *Carlow Stone* is a huge piece of Shap granite, brought by the glacier.

Covering 90 acres, Semerwater today is a popular yachting and water-skiing location, and the haunt of wildfowl; prehistoric lake dwellers have left evidence of settlements, and this may account for various legends which feature the lake. One legend has it that a submerged town may be seen, with luck, from a boat gliding over the still water.

Close to the N shore, the hamlet of *Countersett* has a *Quaker Meeting House* dating from 1710 and still in use. It stands next to *Countersett Old Hall* where George Fox, founder of the Society of Friends, stayed in 1652 when the Hall was new, sleeping in the little room over the front porch. The River Bain, crossed by a bridge as it leaves Semerwater, below Countersett, flows N for 3m to the Ure at Bainbridge. It is said to be the shortest river in England.

**Settle**                                                A3
*Ribblesdale. Town on A65/B6479, 16m NW of Skipton*
Gateway to upper Ribblesdale and the Yorkshire Dales National Park, Settle lies close to some of the finest and most familiar landmarks of the *Craven* district. The town's narrow streets, yards and fine Georgian houses make it a pleasant centre for exploring the moors; Upper Settle has a green, the market square has a 17th-c. *Shambles*, and the *Town Hall* of 1832 is built in the Elizabethan style. The **Museum of North Craven Life** in Victoria Street has folk displays; *Castleberg Crag* high above the market square provides a satisfying panorama over the dale and fells. The A65 leading NW to Ingleton (11m) passes beneath the extraordinary *Giggleswick Scar*, a great, straight limestone wall marking the site of a fault where the land lying on the SW has subsided. With its curious ebbing and flowing well, this is the most impressive of the Craven Faults.

Above Settle on Langcliffe Scar (E) is **Victoria Cave**, with *Jubilee Cave* nearby, where prehistoric relics have been found. Off the B6479 near Stainforth are *Stainforth Force* and *Catrigg Force*; E of the road, Goat Lane leads NE to the head of Littondale. It passes *Pen-y-Ghent* (2273ft), one of the millstone grit-capped 'three peaks', which is skirted by the *Pennine Way*. Pot-holers and climbers find challenge here: *Hull Pot* on the hill's W slope is popular. 1½m past the quarrying village of Horton-in-Ribblesdale on the B6479, a track leads to *South House Pavement Nature Reserve*, near South House Farm. Cared for by the Yorkshire Wildlife Trust, the reserve shows typical plant life of Carboniferous Limestone Pavement on the E slopes of Ingleborough. A smaller road leads to the dale head and wooded *Ling Gill National Nature Reserve* (4½m), also passed by the Pennine Way on its route N to *Hawes*

in Wensleydale. The terrain here, rough and grassy slopes above cliff-like rocks, is difficult but rewarding. The reserve is cared for by the Nature Conservancy Council.

W of Settle, across the Ribble, is the village of *Giggleswick* with its 15th-c. Perpendicular *Church* (St Alkelda). The village is also noted for its public school.

**Sheriff Hutton**                                         C3
*Ryedale. Village off A64, 9m SW of Malton*
Standing on a rise S of the *Howardian Hills*, the craggy outline of the village's castle ruin can be seen from far across the Plain of York. The village has its *Hall* (remodelled in 1732), three small greens, and cottages built of stone from the **Castle**, which still dominates.

The castle was begun in 1382 near the site of Bertram de Bulmer's original 12th-c. stronghold, the *earthworks* of which can be seen just to the S. The castle was later owned by Richard III. There are remains of the corner towers, with some of their impressive tunnel vaulting, and parts of the walls, gatehouse and great hall.

The **Church of St Helen and the Holy Cross** stands E of the village. It was begun in Norman times and added to throughout the Middle Ages. It has some interesting monuments, including a brass with two effigies of the infants Dorothy and John Fenys (d. 1491), wrapped in swaddling clothes. An alabaster effigy of a boy is thought to represent Edward, Prince of Wales, Richard III's only child who died aged 11 at Middleham Castle (1484). In the S aisle is a fine carving of The Last Supper.

**Skelton** see *Newby Hall*

**Skipton**                                                A3
*Airedale. Pop 12,560. 9m W of Ilkley (A59/A65/A629/B6265). EC Tue MD Mon, Wed, Fri, Sat. Inf: Tel (0756) 2809*
Skipton faces the broad valley of the River Aire on its W as the river emerges from the Yorkshire Dales National Park. Hemmed in by moors, Skipton – or 'Sheeptown' – has factories and mills and, rather unusually, four market days when High Street with its wide cobble-stone sidewalks, fully occupied by stalls, attracts the dalesfolk from a wide area. Sloping N, High Street is dominated by Holy Trinity Church and the imposing Castle just beyond.

The **Castle**, one of the most complete in England, was founded in the 11th c., but the building as we see it grew in the 14th c. and the 17th c., and in the Tudor period. All this work was done by the Clifford family, who owned the castle from 1311. Standing on a rocky eminence of about 200ft, this is a superb example of a medieval fortress, entered through a formidable Tudor *Gatehouse* with four round battlemented towers, bearing a quotation from Horace honouring the 3rd Earl of Cumberland. The huge towers of the main core remain, with the *Great Hall* and *Long Gallery* and cobbled courts and lawns, including the picturesque *Conduit Court* with its old oak tree.

The Clifford motto, 'Desormais' ('henceforth') forms the inner and outer parapets of the gateway, and the family coat-of-arms is in the courtyard and at the main entrance. Lady Anne Clifford was born at the castle, and it is with her name that it is chiefly associated, as are other castles throughout the North of England which she restored. Skipton was the principal seat of the family until Lady Anne's death (1676). During the Civil War it was a Royalist stronghold, gallantly defended for three years in spite of great privation.

The 14th-c. **Church of the Holy Trinity** has a magnificent bossed roof of the late 15th c. and a beautiful chancel screen of 1533. The 12th-c. font has an impressive-looking Jacobean cover, octagonal with a spire. The vault of the Clifford family and their monuments are in the sanctuary; Lady Anne Clifford restored the church after devastation suffered in the Civil War, and some of the windows bear her initials and the date 1655.

Apart from church and castle, other attractions for the visitor include old inns and pleasant shops; intriguing ginnels and yards lead down to the *Leeds and Liverpool Canal*. In the holiday months this section forms a marina, with pleasure craft of all shapes and sizes. In Sheep Street are the *stocks* and *Tolbooth*; housed in the Palladian-style *Town Hall* (1862) is the **Craven Museum**, devoted to local archaeology, geology, history, natural history and folk life in the fascinating area of *Craven*. On Chapel Hill on the Grassington road, near the church, is a restored 13th-c. water-powered corn mill with two wheels in operation, driving a variety of machines. There is a *Blacksmith's Forge* in action: the complex is now the **George Leatt Industrial & Folk Museum**.

3m W of Skipton, **Broughton Hall** dates from 1750, although the fabric of the mansion is of the late 16th c. The stable range and the classical wing and entrance are later additions; later still, W. A. Nesfield designed the *Italian Garden* and *Conservatory* (1855). The earliest interior is the *Entrance Hall* of 1750, with columns of imitation marble. The

house can be visited by groups by appointment.

Occupying a steep hillside 14m SE of Skipton is the village of **Haworth**, former home of the Brontë sisters and one of England's foremost literary shrines. The area of interest is atmospheric and compact: a darkly-paved street, West Lane, climbs to the top of the village and a path winds up to the church, from there ascending beside the graveyard with its towering trees to the Parsonage at the edge of the moors.

Built in 1778 of local stone, the *Parsonage* was occupied by the Brontë family from 1820-61. It is now the **Brontë Parsonage Museum**, housing Brontë manuscripts and relics. Furnishing and decorations in the style of the family include Anne's rocking chair and the sofa on which Emily died. Charlotte's shoes and hat are among the personal possessions which fill the rooms; the memorabilia concern all members of the household, including the maidservants.

The *Church of St Michael and All Angels* (rebuilt 1879-81) contains the tombs of two of the Brontë sisters: Charlotte (1816-55) and Emily (1818-48). Other Brontë associations are to be seen in West Lane, notably *The Black Bull Hotel* in which Branwell Brontë succumbed to alcoholism. The street with its tea rooms and souvenir shops is closed to traffic: from the bottom of the street the view is of slate-roofed houses and factory chimneys over the neighbouring hillside.

In the area of Haworth there are many walks across the moors which inspired the sisters, with features which occur in their novels. The *Brontë Waterfall* (2m W) is a particular attraction.

## Sledmere House D3

*Humberside. Historic house on B1253 (B1251/B1252), 11m SE of Malton*

Situated deep in the *Yorkshire Wolds*, this restored Georgian house is the ancestral home of the Sykes family whose enclosing of the Wolds sheep pastures in the 18th c. encouraged a widespread return of this fertile chalkland to arable farmland.

The present building was enlarged in 1786-90 by Sir Christopher Sykes, the argricultural pioneer, to his own design; the original building of 1751 replaced a Tudor house. A fire in 1911 destroyed much of the building (only the outer walls, dairy and laundry survived) and it was rebuilt from original drawings and plasterwork moulds, notably those of Joseph Rose who contributed interior decorations in the Adam style.

The contents, including Chippendale and Sheraton furniture, paintings, porcelain and antique statuary, were also saved and are now on view. Notable also is the *Turkish Room*, created in this century, which is a copy of a tiled apartment in the Valideh Mosque in Cairo, and the 100ft *Library*, which occupies one whole side of the house on the first floor. 'Capability' Brown's 200-acre *Gardens* and *Park* were created for Sir Christopher at the expense of the then existing village, which was removed and rebuilt to make space. A special feature of Sledmere is the *Italian Garden*, with its fountain and 18th-c. copies of Antique statues.

Sir Christopher's son Sir Tatton Sykes was a well-known local figure who continued the tradition of innovatory farming methods and established the Sledmere stud, among other entrepreneurial activities. The 2nd Sir Tatton made his impact by restoring and rebuilding village churches throughout the Wolds to the designs of G.E. Street. Temple Moore rebuilt *St Mary's Church* (1893) in the grounds, with the exception of the 14th-c. tower which was only partially restored. The church is considered one of the finest of its period in England, with elaborate carving by John Baker. The neat village shaded by beeches has various monuments commemorating the Sykes family, including the well-known *Waggoner's Memorial* on the green. This commemorates the Yorkshire Waggoners, the regiment raised by Sir Mark Sykes in 1912. SE of the village on *Garton Hill*, a *monument* to the first Sir Tatton commands a memorable view of the Wolds.

About 6m W, and reached by footpath from *Wharram-le-Street* along the Birdsall road, is the site of *Wharram Percy*, a well-known example of a deserted medieval village which like other such sites reflects the early history of the region. Now surrounded by fertile farmland, the location shows little besides its roofless Church (*St Martin's*); regular excavations have revealed evidence of the village's desertion at the time of the Black Death (*c* 1350), of its later repopulation and its final desertion in the early 16th c. when peasants' arable farming strips were turned over to sheep grazing by landowners.

About ½m SW of Wharram-le-Street off the Birdsall road is the Yorkshire Wildlife Trust's *Wharram Quarry Nature Reserve*, showing common chalk plants on the quarry floor and cliff face and, some years, bee orchids. A good variety of butterflies is found here.

## Slingsby                                    C2
*Ryedale. Village off B1257, 6m NW of Malton*

Slingsby's limestone houses, cottages and attractive green with its maypole are dominated by All Saints' Church and the castle, both of which stand at the NW end of the village.

The *Castle* is something of a misnomer since the building is the partly-completed, 17th-c. fortified and moated house of the Cavendish family, probably built on the site of a medieval fort. The *Church*, rebuilt in the 1860s, has parts of a medieval structure incorporated into the Victorian building. Inside rests the villager, Wyville by name, who according to legend, 'with his dog, did kill a monstrous serpent that lived and preyed on passengers on the road to Malton'. 1m from the village and not far S of the road, an old gravel pit is said to have been the monster's lair.

## Snape                                       B2
*N Yorks. Village off B6268, 3m NE of Masham*

This is a pleasant little village of red-roofed cottages straggling alongside a green, situated near the E end of Wensleydale. It is noteworthy for its 12th-c. *Castle*, partly ruined and partly inhabited, which is approached along a park-like avenue of lime trees. Its chapel, dating from the 15th c., is now **St Mary's Church**.

The castle is especially interesting for its association with Catherine Parr, who was to become Henry VIII's sixth and last wife, and who worshipped regularly in the little chapel which is reached by a flight of stairs. Its stucco ceiling bears traces of painting attributed to the 17th-c. Neopolitan artist, Antonio Verrio; on the walls are beautiful carvings of the Stations of the Cross, and the windows contain fine medieval glass.

Close to the village, **Thorp Perrow Arboretum** has 60 acres of landscaped grounds with a picnic area, and a collection of over 2000 species of shrubs and trees including some of the largest and rarest in England.

## Staithes                                    C1
*N Yorks. Village off A174. 10m NW of Whitby*

The modern village lies close to the main road. At the bottom of the steep hill is the *Harbour*, protected by twin breakwaters and a pair of massive headlands. The well-known **Cod and Lobster Inn**, shuttered against storms, is close to the cottage where Captain Cook lived whilst he was apprenticed to Mr Sanderson, a draper and grocer.

From here the fishing village straggles up the hillside, cleft by a deep valley through which flows *Roxby Beck*; this part is especially favoured by artists and photographers (the painter Dame Laura Knight lived and worked in Staithes for some years). The cottages, inns and shops are mostly of grey stone and have a rather sombre appearance, particularly as they huddle closely together at irregular intervals, the blocks divided one from another by steep little alleyways suitable only for pedestrian traffic. The foreshore echoes this grey in its black-grey shale. Motorised vehicles are confined to the narrow street which connects the harbour area with the community on the hilltop. Parking by the shore is limited, and it is advisable to use the car park near the main road.

Once a thriving fishing village (and a smuggling centre), Staithes is still the home of fishermen; also of workers in the industrial towns further N. 'Staithes bonnets', which used to be everyday headgear for the womenfolk, are remembered, and some can still be seen.

N of the village are **Boulby Cliffs**, now part of industrial Cleveland, at 666ft the highest cliffs in England. The *Cleveland Way* passes through the village.

## Stokesley                                            C1
*N Yorks. Town on A172/A173/B1257, 3m SW of Great Ayton. EC Wed MD Fri*

The recently-opened bypass has made this charming market town a quiet backwater, and enhanced its 18th-c. appearance. It stands by the River Leven, which is crossed by a pack-horse bridge and by other, narrow footbridges. Running E-W and parallel with the river is the long, broad market place, which further W becomes High Street, flanked by Georgian houses on either side and occupied by central islands on one of which stands the *Town Hall* (1853). Opposite is the *Manor House*, now Council Offices, and behind that the *Church of St Peter and St Paul* with its 15th-c. chancel and tower, and 18th-c. nave.

W of High Street, other pleasant houses edge the grass and trees of West Green. Here the handsome *Handyside House*, with a pedimented doorway, faces the town. Other attractive features of Stokesley include old inns and shops, *Shambles* and *Butter Market*, and the tree-lined riverside walk.

The B1257 leading S through *Bilsdale* to Helmsley (18m) passes Forestry Commission picnic areas and trails, and there are good views over the moors.

**Studley Royal Park** see *Fountains Abbey*

## Stump Cross Caverns                                  B3
*Nidderdale. On B6265, 5m W of Pateley Bridge*

The famous Stump Cross Caverns form a remarkably beautiful and impressive chain of limestone chambers extending for a considerable distance into the face of Greenhow Hill and adorned with hundreds of *stalactites* and *stalagmites*. The caverns are well lighted, and a visit is an interesting and unusual experience: in England their only rivals probably being the Wookey complex in the Cheddar Gorge.

Two lead miners came across the caves in 1860, and a survey was done in 1903; since then there have been other discoveries, including one of five reindeer skeletons. Many of the caverns have fanciful names – 'Baby's Cradle', 'Sand Castles', 'Snow Drift', 'Sentinel' – which aptly describe their appearance. Most spectacular is the *'Cathedral'*, about 40ft wide and 122ft high, with stalactites arranged like organ pipes.

Local mining history goes back as far as the Bronze Age and disused mine workings abound on the moors between Grassington and Pateley Bridge. The village of *Greenhow* (E), over 1300 ft, has superb and far-reaching views.

## Sutton Bank                                          C2
*Ryedale. Viewpoint on A170, 8m W of Helmsley. Inf: Tel (0845) 597426*

Where the Hambleton Hills drop abruptly to the Plain of York the road traverses Sutton Bank, and in about ½m descends some 500ft by 1-in-4 gradients and acute bends towards the village of *Sutton-under-Whitestone Cliff*. From the bank (960ft) is a magnificent view encompassing the plain as far as the Pennines; the bank itself is a prominent landmark for miles around. At the top is a *North Yorkshire Moors* National Park Information Centre with an exhibition and other facilities; the headquarters of the Yorkshire Gliding Club is situated between here and *Roulston Scar* (S), and the aerobatic activities of the club members add drama to the scene.

A little way W along this famous escarpment, below the sheer face of *Whitestone Cliff*, is **Gormire**, a mysterious lake with no apparent outlet or inlet, said to be bottomless. Clifftop and lakeside show a variety of plant and animal habitats in the Yorkshire Wildlife Trust's *Garbutt Wood Nature Reserve*. From the top of the bank, the *Cleveland Way* runs N, following the line of the Hambleton Hills to Osmotherley; a spur of this long-distance walk extends to Roulston Scar and the White Horse, which can also be reached from *Kilburn below.

## Swaledale A2
*N Yorks. Dale in Yorkshire Dales National Park*
Northernmost dale in the Yorkshire Dales National Park, Swaledale is narrow and winding in its upper reaches, opening up wild and ruggedly picturesque scenery which embraces lofty moors, steep-sided fells, huddled greystone villages and impressive patches of rock and woodland. Between Reeth and Richmond the dale becomes verdant; the river approaches Richmond through a rocky gorge. Below Richmond it changes from a fast-flowing, at times turbulent, stream and leaves Swaledale as a placid, quietly-running water to flow across the rich agricultural land of the Plain of York. It joins the Ure to form the Ouse, just below Myton-on-Swale, E of Boroughbridge.

The river rises at the edge of the National Park on the Cumbria border, a few miles SE of Kirkby Stephen. Draining 576 sq m of varying Yorkshire countryside, the Swale's length of 83m makes it Yorkshire's longest river. A spur of the National Park follows the dale E to Richmond.

*Keld in its amphitheatre of fells is the highest village in the dale. Striking moorland scenery surrounds *Buttertubs Pass* on the moorland road running S from Thwaite into Wensleydale (see *Hawes). The dale with its drystone boundary walls, stone farmhouses and field barns for wintering cattle is well seen from the pass; to the W of the pass is Great Shunner Fell, over which the *Pennine Way* climbs from Wensleydale to Thwaite.

**Tabular Hills** see *North Yorkshire Moors*

## Thirsk B2
*N Yorks. Town on A61/A168/A170/B1448. 9m SE of Northallerton. EC Wed MD Mon, Sat. Inf: Tel (0845) 22755*
Thirsk was important in the Viking period, and features in the Domesday Book. A castle stood here in early medieval days and its owner, Robert de Mowbray, is remembered in the name of the fertile *Vale of Mowbray* which extends N below the Hambleton Hills. To the NE stretch the *North Yorkshire Moors*, and the National Park.

Even more than the Dales market towns, Thirsk seems to have retained the aura of its time as a well-known posting station; few towns of its size can have more coaching inns. With its 18th-c. houses, small but attractive shops, narrow streets, cobbled market place

and clock tower, the impression is almost Dickensian. Oldest of the inns is *The Three Tuns*, once the Manor House; the handsome *Hall*, built in the 1720s and extended 50 years later by John Carr, stands near the church.

**St Mary's Church** is a superb example of the Perpendicular style. Building began in 1430 after an endowment of chantry, and carried on until the 16th c., and the church is considered the best of its period in Yorkshire. It was sympathetically restored by G.E. Street in 1877. Its dark stone and buttressed tower are offset by a lacy parapet which follows the outline of the church. The nave has a fine wagon roof; there is a modest brass memorial to Robert Thirsk, founder of the chantry (d 1419) and faded 17th-c. paintings of the apostles on the clerestory walls.

The church stands near the water meadows of the Cod Beck, where there are pleasant walks. The town has become something of a place of pilgrimage for followers of the Herriot cult, for whom Thirsk is 'Darrowby': Herriot's own *Veterinary Premises* are a magnetic draw. His real-life marriage took place in St Mary's. (See also *Herriot Country.) Thomas Lord, founder of Lord's cricket ground in London, was born here in 1755; his house in Kirkgate has the **Thirsk Museum**, with cricketing memorabilia and local history displays.

4m E off the A170 is **Osgodby Hall**, a small Jacobean manor house with a fine 17th-c. forecourt and staircase, still a family home.

## Thornton Dale C2
*Ryedale. Village on A170, 2m E of Pickering*
This beautiful showpiece of a village suffers from a surfeit of traffic during the tourist season, but with its small tree-shrouded green, market cross and stocks, it still retains an old-world charm. Thornton Beck flows down from Dalby Forest, alongside a tree-lined lane past a famous *Thatched Cottage*, possibly the most photographed building for miles around. It then continues under a bridge, alongside the main road to the green, then out towards Malton. Cottages and houses are approached by white-painted wooden bridges over the beck, there are many cafés and gift shops, and a row of *Almshouses* dated 1656. The Jacobean *Hall* is an old persons' home.

The Decorated **All Saints' Church** stands near the bridge. Its chancel dates from 1866. In the churchyard is the grave of Matthew Grimes, who was one of Napoleon's guards on St Helena and officiated at the Emperor's funeral.

3m NE of the village in **Dalby Forest**, the *Dalby Forest Drive* (toll) follows a 9m route to Bickley, 3m W of Hackness. The drive is maintained by the Forestry Commission; its **Visitor Centre** at Low Dalby includes displays of wildlife and forestry and provides information about the numerous picnic areas and waymarked walks along the route. (See also *North Yorkshire Forests*.)

The walks vary in length from 1m to the 16m walk from *Reasty Bank* (see *Hackness*). A spectacular viewpoint is reached on the *Cross Cliff View Walk*; from *Staindale Lake*, created by the FC in 1976, access can be obtained to the **Bridestones** (NT) via a National Trust and Yorkshire Wildlife Trust *Trail* leading across a *Nature Reserve* and moorland. These free-standing rocks have been eroded and weathered from Jurassic sandstone into fantastic shapes, some looking like huge mushrooms. Many isolated outcrops on these moors are known as bridestones, and the word is thought to derive from the Norse meaning of 'brink', or 'edge' stones. From here, other paths lead to places with fascinating names like Needle Point, Bridestones Griff and Dovedale Griff – 'griff' being a local term for small ravines scoured out of becks.

### Thwaite                                                    A2
*Swaledale. Village on B6270, 9m W of Reeth*

Surrounded by high fells and undisturbed moorland country, this quiet village was the birthplace in the 19th c. of Richard and Cherry Kearton, pioneers of the popularisation of natural history by books and films. Cherry began by taking photographs to illustrate Richard's books, and he took the first motion pictures of a wild bird in 1903. These talented brothers went to school at *Muker*, 1m E.

S of Thwaite, a lonely moorland road ascends by way of the celebrated *Buttertubs Pass* to *Hawes* in Wensleydale; W of the pass the *Pennine Way* crosses to Thwaite via Great Shunner Fell. Another moorland route leads into Wensleydale from the road between Muker and Ivelet, and affords magnificent views. The tree-shaded hump-back bridge is the prettiest in the dale.

### Topcliffe                                                  B2
*N Yorks. Village on A167, 5m SW of Thirsk*

Here the River Swale rushes over a weir and flows under a twin-arched bridge.
**St Columba's Church** is an early Victorian representation of the Decorated style, and is interesting for the fine specimen of 14th-c. Flemish brasswork which shows Thomas

Topcliffe (d. 1362) and his wife (d. 1391), protected by canopies of foliage and angels clutching censers and musical instruments, and with a couple of deities each holding a soul wrapped in a shroud. Probably the most interesting part of the brass is actually hidden from view, since on the reverse side is an engraving of a ship; this is believed to be the oldest brass in England to have such a decoration. The church has other interesting monuments, and a window by Edward Burne-Jones when young.

1m downstream are the ancient earthworks known as **Maiden Bower**, comprising a motte and bailey. A timber castle was constructed here as his first English home by William de Percy (1071), who fought at the Battle of Hastings. William founded the Percy dynasty of Northumberland, and ultimately the Dukedom of that county with its family seat at Alnwick Castle.

### Vale of Mowbray see *Thirsk*

### Vale of Pickering                                          C2
*Ryedale. Between A64 & A170*

This well-defined broad alluvial plain was in prehistoric times a huge glacial lake; evidence of lake-dwellers has been discovered in what is now green and fertile agricultural land.

The vale extends E from the Plain of York, contained by the Yorkshire Wolds along its S edge and the North Yorkshire Moors on its N. The vale's W boundary is formed by the Hambleton and the Howardian Hills, really one long S-N range: the Hambletons form the North Yorkshire Moors' steep W flank, while from their foot the gentle Howardians continue in a curve to contain the vale's SW corner. This is breached by the *Kirkham Gorge* running N-S between the Howardian Hills and the Yorkshire Wolds.

The River Derwent rises on the moors above the coast and flows S along *Forge Valley* to the vale, which it waters from E-W before flowing S through the Kirkham Gorge to the Plain of York. Ancient channels of communication run from *York* through the gorge to the Roman town of *Malton*, which lies at the SE corner of the Howardian Hills, commanding gorge and vale.

The gorge was cut by waters from the lake that once filled Pickering Vale's basin; the water was cut off from the North Sea by ice-sheets and glacial boulder-clay. This material still forms the higher land between the vale and its E boundary, the coast between *Scarborough* and Filey Brigg.

The site of the *Starr Carr Mesolithic Lake Dwellings* is in the E of the vale, on private land off the A64, 2m SE of *Seamer*. Excavations have yielded evidence of stilt dwellings, a wooden jetty and forest clearings where herbs and vegetables were grown.

## Wade's Causeway see *Cawthorn Roman Camps*

## Wensley
B2

*Wensleydale. Village on A684, 2m SW of Leyburn*

Wensley was the first of the dale's market towns, its charter being granted in 1202; its importance was recognized by the bestowal of its name on the only principal dale not named after its river. A disastrous year of plague in 1563, and later the granting of a charter to Askrigg in the higher dale, ended the town's importance.

The village which surrounds the green provides the main entrance to 17th-c. *Bolton Hall*, the seat of Lord Bolton since neighbouring Bolton Castle's demise in the Civil War. The Hall was partially rebuilt after a disastrous fire in 1902. The 3rd Duke of Bolton's wife was Lavinia Fenton, the original Polly Peachum in John Gay's *The Beggars' Opera*. She used to entertain guests at the Hall by singing from the top of a watch-tower on Penhill 2½m across the dale, and the structure eventually became known as '*Polly Peachum's Tower*'. Not to be outshone by Lavinia, the Duke had the family pew in the church built to resemble a box at the Theatre Royal, Drury Lane, complete with curtains and cushioned seats.

The Scrope family pew incorporates parts of a fine 16th-c. rood screen thought to be from Easby Abbey, and is one of a collection of interesting items to be seen in *Holy Trinity Church*. This splendid church dates from the 13th c. and shows elements of each of the following five centuries in its architecture. The church has a wooden reliquary which is thought to have held St Agatha's bones, and traces of a wall painting of the *Three Quick and the Three Dead* (c. 1330). There is a memorial to Peter Goldsmith, the surgeon who attended the mortally wounded Nelson on *HMS Victory* at the Battle of Trafalgar, and who is buried in the churchyard.

## Wensleydale
B2

*N Yorks. Dale in Yorkshire Dales National Park*

This is the only one of the five principal dales in the Yorkshire Dales National Park not named after its river, but after one of the villages (once a market town) about halfway along the river's course. The splendid

pastoral scenery leaves the impression that it is probably the most calm and serene of the dales, given less to diversity and extremes than any of its neighbours.

The dale's river is the Ure, 68m long and watering an area of 391 sq m. It rises E of the Settle-Carlisle railway at its highest point near Aisgill, in Cumbria. Flowing down to Hawes and through *Aysgarth*, the river rushes over a series of *waterfalls* before entering the lower dale at Wensley; it then passes through rolling pastureland and leaves the dale at Jervaulx, continuing SE to Masham, Ripon and Boroughbridge to join the Swale below Aldborough, the combined waters forming the Ouse.

As in other dales, a thriving modern industry is tourism; dairying and horse breeding are traditional industries that have survived, while on the moors mining has left its relics next to the earthworks and tumuli of prehistoric Dales people. Ancient field systems can still be seen outlined on the hillsides around Bolton Castle and other parts of the dale, and Wensleydale sheep graze the fells. Relics of the wool and hand-knitting industries that flourished from medieval times until last century can be seen in the folk museum at *Hawes*.

## West Burton
A2

*Wensleydale. Village on B6160, 2m SE of Aysgarth*

West Burton, on Walden Beck under the NW flank of Penhill, has a large oblong green, and is one of the most attractive villages in Wensleydale. In the village is *Flanders Hall* (1779), and the *Cauldron Falls* can be seen just downstream.

The beck flows down from Buckden Pike (SW) to join Bishopdale Beck below the village, and the united stream flows into the River Ure. Towering above the village is *Penhill* (1792ft), a flat-topped landmark conspicuous for miles around, particularly when viewed from the N side of the dale.

## West Tanfield
B2

*N Yorks. Village on A6108, 6m NW of Ripon*

The bridge carrying the main road over the River Ure provides a much photographed view of the village. Nothing remains of the mansion of the great Marmion family, immortalised by Sir Walter Scott, except the 15th-c. *Gatehouse Tower* with an oriel window and ancient fireplaces, which stands next to the **Church of St Nicholas**. Originally a Norman structure, the church was rebuilt in the Decorated-Perpendicular style probably about the time the Marmion homestead was erected. The family tombs are in the N aisle which was rebuilt in 1343 by Maude de Marmion. Erected over one of the tombs is an ancient iron hearse for the hanging of a pall; the uprights are spiked for the placement of candles, and it is believed to be the only one of its kind in Britain.

There are also curiosities in the church, notably some interesting carving. The pulpit stairway shows St Nicholas with three children in a tub; the lectern has monks playing a flute, horn, violin and harp, and the poppyhead stalls display a variety of animals and birds. There are also carvings by the 'mouseman' of *Kilburn*, Robert Thompson.

1m NE of the Church are the *Thornborough Circles*, three Neolithic-Bronze Age henges in varying states of preservation, and groups of Bronze Age barrows of which one, when excavated in the 19th c., yielded a tree-trunk coffin and artefacts.

## West Witton                                     A2

*Wensleydale. Village on A684, 4m W of Leyburn. Event: Burning of 'Owd Bartle' (1st Sat after Aug 24)*

An ungainly village straddling its long main street, West Witton is not to be compared with East Witton lower downstream. It is of interest, however, because of the quaint annual ceremony of the burning of 'Owd Bartle' which takes place on the Saturday after St Bartholomew's Day. The *Church* is dedicated to the Saint, but this does not appear to have any bearing on the custom which consists of carrying an effigy of 'Owd Bartle' in procession down the street, stopping at various points for the reciting of a verse of doggerel:

At Penhill Crags he tore his rags,
At Hunter's Thorn he blew his horn.
At Capplebank Stee he brake his knee,
At Grisgill Beck he brake his neck,
At Wadham's End he couldn't fend,
At Grisgill End he made his end.

At Grass Gill End (Grisgill) 'Owd Bartle' is burned on a bonfire and merrymaking goes on well into the night.

## Wharfedale                                     A3/B3

*N Yorks. Dale in Yorkshire Dales National Park*

Wharfedale's scenery ranges from the bleak moorland of the upper reaches to the flat, fertile farmlands of the Plain of York. In between is some of the finest limestone landscape in Britain, giving way to millstone grit between Grassington and Burnsall. Each rock type gives rise to particular plant species which appear in great profusion and variety, making the dale a botanists' paradise. Hikers, climbers and cavers also find reward here.

The river is 75m long and drains an area of 394 sq m. It starts its journey in wild and beautiful uplands at the head of *Langstrothdale*, where Oughtershaw and Greenfield Becks converge at Beckermonds. Turning SE, it enters the broader valley of Wharfedale just below *Hubberholme*. ½m before *Kilnsey Crag* is reached, the broadening dale is joined by the tributary dale *Littondale* (NW), lonely and remote.

Below this point the river flows through the woods and pastures which make the renowned setting of *Bolton Abbey*; it then leaves the Park and flows through *Ilkley*, *Otley*, Wetherby and Tadcaster to join the Ouse near Cawood.

**Wharram Percy** see *Sledmere House*

## Whitby                                     D1

*N Yorks. Pop 12,710. 20m NW of Scarborough (A171/A174). Events: Planting of the Penny Hedge (day before Ascension Day); Music, Drama and Arts Festival (Jun); Regatta (3rd week in Aug); Folk Festival (week before Summer Bank Hol). EC Wed MD Mon, Wed. Inf: Tel (0947) 602674*

Overlooked by the skeletal remains of its abbey, this ancient port and modern holiday resort is superbly situated on steep cliffs at the mouth of the River Esk, on the edge of the *North Yorkshire Moors*. The old town by the E Cliff is connected to the newer part on the W Cliff by a swing bridge which has to be opened to allow all but the smallest vessels to reach the upper harbour. It is here that the commercial wharf is situated, handling continental vessels principally carrying cargoes of timber; a *marina* accommodates a large number of yachts and other pleasure craft during the holiday season, and there is a small boat-building yard.

Whitby has been a fishing town since medieval times; in the 17th c. the port handled alum from local mine works, and by the 18th c. it had become an important whaling centre. The legacy of these days can be seen in the town's Georgian buildings, notably in terraces climbing the W Cliff. Victorian industry made Whitby famous for jet; the railway (1847) brought seaside development along the W Cliff.

Both cliffs rise steeply from the harbour and present a picturesque appearance of brick and red-roofed houses honeycombed by ginnels, known as 'ghauts'. In the older town near the swing bridge is Grape Lane with a plaque marking **Captain Cook's House**, where he lodged while apprenticed to the shipowner John Walker. It was ships built in boat yards bordering the *Harbour* close by that the great navigator used for his explorations. Near the harbourside at the end of Pier Road is the **Whitby Lifeboat Museum**, where local lifeboat history and wreck diorama can be seen. Also on view is the last rowing lifeboat of the RNLI.

On the E Cliff, standing at the top of 199 steps, is St Mary's Church; dominating the town from the clifftop beyond are the windswept remains of the **Abbey** originally founded by St Hilda in 657. Here in 664 the Abbess presided over the Synod of Whitby, called by King Oswy of Northumbria, at which the rites and authority of the Roman Church were adopted in preference to those of the Celtic Church, and the method of determining the date of Easter settled. The early monastery which housed men and women was probably made of wood and was destroyed by the Danes in 867. The abbey was re-established in 1078 and parts still remain of that period, but the present weathered sandstone ruin dates from the 13th and 14th c.

The 12th-c. **St Mary's Church** has undergone many alterations between the Norman and Georgian periods, but was never 'restored' in the 19th c. It is a remarkable building with many intriguing features, notably the many galleries inside, and the 17th-c. roof constructed by ships' carpenters in cabin style. The furnishings reflect the informality of the architecture: there are box pews, a three-decker pulpit and innumerable memorial tablets, many to seafarers who lie at rest inside the church as well as in the churchyard, where many of the tombstones are so weatherworn as to be featureless. At the top of the 199 steps is *Caedmon's Cross*, a memorial to England's first recorded Christian poet, who lived at the abbey.

Rising steeply beside the steps is the '*donkey road*', a narrow cobbled way once used by pack animals. Between the church and abbey, the ancient *Abbey Cross* stands in a car park. For those who climb the steps, there is a fine view across the harbour to the W Cliff and Sandsend, and up-river towards the village of Ruswarp. From the church there is a 1m walk SE along the cliff path (part of the Cleveland Way) to **Saltwick Nab**, a 7½-acre NT property jutting into the sea; by doubling the distance, *Whitby High Light* and *Fog Signal* are reached. At the bottom of the church steps, Church Street leads S past Market Place to Grape Lane and the bridge. The lower harbour is protected by two stone piers with lighthouses, joined by bridges to extension piers constructed of stone and timber and each also with a lighthouse.

On the W Cliff are the bus and railway stations, amusement and shopping areas, hotels and guest houses. On the headland high above the harbour is a *statue* of Captain Cook and a *whalebone arch*, with a plaque describing the town's whaling industry and the exploits of local whaling captains and Arctic explorers William Scoresby (father and son), who operated from here in the 19th c. The *Spa Pavilion and Theatre* and *Royal Crescent Gardens* are situated on the Promenade, where there is also a cliff lift to a sandy beach. Near the shopping and business centre on the SW side of town, **Pannett Park** has gardens sloping down the side of a steep ravine. Here the **Pannet Park Museum and Art Gallery** contains a mass of exhibits, many devoted to seafaring, whaling and Captain Cook. An interesting section belonging to the Whitby Literary and Philosophical Society holds local records and documents. At the bottom of Flowergate, near the bridge, is the **Sutcliffe Gallery** where original prints of the 19th-c. photographer Frank Meadows Sutcliffe can be seen. They show rural and maritime scenes; reproductions are on sale in the shop.

A connection with the more recent past is that of the writer, Bram Stoker, who, while staying here at the end of the last century, was inspired by St Mary's churchyard and the abbey ruin to begin his novel, *Dracula*. A 'Dracula' trail from the W cliff ends here. The jet trade continues in a modest form, the raw material being obtained from the local cliffs and scars which are also rewarding for the geologist. Whitby is also well known for production of the typical fishing boat, the coble, for traditional methods of curing kippers, and for the hand-knitting of fishermen's 'gansys' (guernseys). A more recently-developed craft is glass model making.

Whitby has all the traditional seaside amusements, including boating and fishing; its beautiful surrounding scenery varies from wild moors and coastal cliffs to the forests and pastures of Esk Dale. The stretch of river between the villages of *Ruswarp* and *Sleights* is an idyllic place for boating and canoeing, with embankment cafés set in gardens. A recent addition to the small craft is an 'African Queen' style steam boat complete with awning and immaculate brasswork.

There are Forestry Commission waymarked walks and picnic areas around **Falling Foss** 5m S, reached from the B1416 running S from Ruswarp to Fylingdales Moor. Situated in a wooded valley on Little Beck, a tributary of the Esk, this attractive waterfall drops 30ft into a deep, rocky basin. The walks can be followed from *Falling Foss* car park or from *May Beck* car park. The *Cleveland Way* also passes through Whitby, *en route* to Robin Hood's Bay.

Close by is *Newton House Field Centre*, built in the 18th c. as a shooting lodge and occupied since 1967 by the British Young Naturalists' Association; details of courses can be obtained from the Director, Larpool Hall, Whitby. A curiosity near the centre is an enormous boulder (known as *The Hermitage*), hollowed out by a local mason who also carved the two seats on top. The inscription 'GC 1790' over the entrance is believed to refer to George Chubb, a local schoolmaster associated with the building of Newton House.

Information and publications about the North York Moors National Park can be obtained from the *Tourist Information Centre* in New Quay Road.

**White Scar Caves** see *Ingleton*

**Wolds Way**                                    C2/C3/D2
*N Yorks & Humberside. Long-distance footpath*
The Wolds Way, the 12th long-distance path to be designated, was opened on October 2, 1982. It is 80m long and is a continuation of the *Cleveland Way*, starting at *Filey* and turning SW to follow the scythe-shape of the Yorkshire Wolds inland until it reaches the N bank of the Humber at Hessle (5m W of Hull).

**Yorkshire Dales National Park**
*N Yorks*
Designated in 1954, the Park is the third largest of the 10 National Parks in England and Wales and encompasses an area of 680 sq m. It is roughly bounded on the W by Sedbergh and Ingleton, on the S by Settle and Skipton, on the E from Skipton *via* Bolton Abbey to Richmond, with two large indentations W towards Kettlewell and, further N, towards Redmire. A considerable bulge N connects Richmond *via* Tan Hill above Keld to Sedbergh.

The Park covers a territory of wide, sweeping upland moors, cut by deep pastoral valleys with delightful river systems including most of North Yorkshire's western dales: *Swaledale*, *Wensleydale*, upper *Wharfedale*, Malhamdale (above *Airedale*) and *Ribblesdale*; on the W boundary, places like Sedbergh and Dentdale with natural features like Cauldron Snout were taken into Cumbria in the local government reorganisation in 1974.

The Park includes some of the finest limestone scenery in Britain, including the strikingly characterstic landscapes of the *Craven* district with the peaks of Whernside, Ingleborough and Pen-y-Ghent near Ingleton and Settle. The *Pennine Way* and *Dalesway* long-distance footpaths pass through the Park. Centres providing information services and displays illustrating themes of local interest are at *Hawes*, *Aysgarth*, *Grassington*, *Malham* and Clapham near *Ingleton*. There is also a centre at Sedbergh in Cumbria.

**Yorkshire Wolds**
*Humberside*
This scythe-shaped range of chalk hills – a continuation of southern England's chalk uplands – curves round from its SW limit on the River Humber to outcrop in the NE in the cliffs of *Flamborough Head*. The range along its N escarpment dips down to the Vale of Pickering and is riven with deep valleys carrying streams. There are spectacular views over the vale, and across the narrow Kirkham Gorge through which the Derwent flows N-S to the Plain of York, separating the Wolds from the NW ranging Howardian Hills.

At the North Yorkshire cornerstones of this high, oddly-shaped tableland are Norton (near *Malton*) at its NW, and *Filey* on the E coast.

Reaching 808ft at its highest point, *Garrowby Top*, the countryside is quiet and rural in character; with sweeping views over fertile farmland; many valleys created by glacial action are without water, since the streams have long since been absorbed into the chalk. There is much evidence of prehistoric settlement on these hills, and the region today has many attractive woodlands and villages.

The sites of deserted medieval villages deep in the countryside recall the region's history of depredations at the hands of William the Conqueror during his harrying of the North, and in the 14th c. through the Black Death; later the arable strips worked by villagers were seized by the landowners at a time when the land was wanted for sheep pasture. In the 18th c., landowners like the Sykes family of *Sledmere House* returned the land to cultivation, building neat farmsteads sheltered by plantations of trees.

The Wolds are not so open to recreational pursuits as are the moorland and dales parks, N and W; the *Wolds Way*, however, introduces wayfarers to quiet villages and remote farms.

# Index

*Places with entries in the alphabetical Gazetteer are listed in this index only if they also appear elsewhere in the book. Page numbers in bold type indicate the most extensive treatment of the index entry; page numbers in italics indicate illustration*

Adam, Robert 61, 73
Airedale 4-5, **40**
Aislabie, John 57, 58
Aislabie, William 57, 82
Alcuin 28
Aldborough 8, 16, **40**
Alfred the Great 82
Ampleforth Abbey 14, **41**
Appletreewick 15, **41**
Aram, Eugene 69, 78
Aske, Robert 11
Aysgarth 14, 16, 17, **42**
Aylesbury, Earl of 55

Baker, John 87
Baltimore, 2nd Lord 20, 45
Barden Tower 16, **42**
Barry, Charles 61
Bedale 14, **42-3**
Bempton Cliffs 17, 18, **43**
Beningbrough Hall 14, 15, **43**
Bishopthorpe Palace 38
Bodley, G. F. 84
Bolton, Lord 91
Bolton Abbey 14, 16, 17 **44**, *47*
Bolton Castle 11, 16, **44-5**
Bolton-on-Swale 14,15, **45**
Borgnis, Giuseppe 81
Boroughbridge 12, 16, **45**
Boulby Cliffs 18, **88**
Bridestones 18, 64, **90**
Bridlington 14, 15, 16, **46**
Brimham Rocks 17, **46**
Broderick, Cuthbert 83
Brontë, Anne 20, 84, 86
Brontë, Charlotte 82, 86
Brontë family 20, 86
Broughton Hall 15, **86**
Brown, Lancelot 'Capability' 61, 81, 87
Bruce, Robert 74
Bruis, Robert de 60
Buckingham, George Villiers, 2nd Duke of 20, 43, 68
Bulmer, Bertram de 85
Burges, William 58, 73
Burlington, Earl of 37
Burne-Jones, Sir Edward 48, 90
Burton Agnes Hall 14, 16, **48**
Butler, Samuel 79
Buttertubs Pass 18, **63**
Byland Abbey 7, 16, **48**

Carr, John 35, 36, 42, 61, 66, 70, 80, 89
Carr, Rev. William 44
Cartimandua, Queen 40
Castle Howard 6, *12*, 13, 14, 15, **48-9**
Castles, Ruins, Monuments & Ancient Sites 16
Castleton 16, **49**
Catterick 8
Catterick Bridge 16, **49**
Cavendish, Lord Frederick 44
Cavendish family 87
Cawthorn Roman Camps 16, **49**
Cayley, Sir George 20, 84
Cedd, Bishop 60, 69
Charles I 12, 20, 29, 34, 38
Chevin 18, **76**
Chippendale, Thomas 6, 20, 66, 70, 73, 77
Chubb, George 94
Churches 14
Clapham 18, **66**
Clifford, Lady Anne 20, 42, 86
Clifford, Henry, Lord 42
Clifford family 85-6
Clitherow, Margaret 20, 29, 34
Constable Burton Hall 15, 70
Constantius Chlorus 28
Constantine the Great 20, 28
Cook, Captain James 6, 13, 20, 59-60, 87, 92
Coverdale, Miles 20, 52 56
Cow and Calf Rocks 18, **65**
Cowley, Bill 71
Coxwold 14, 15, **52-3**
Cradock, Rear-Admiral Sir Christopher 20, 80
Cromwell, Oliver 12, 20, 45, 53, 72, 81
Cromwell, Richard 67

Dalby Forest 17, **90**
Danby 16, **53**
Danes' Dyke 57
Devonshire, Duke of 44
Dropping Well 18, **69**
Duncombe, Sir Charles 63
Duncombe, Thomas, III 81
Duncombe Park 15, 63

Easby Abbey 14, 16, **53-5**
Edmund, King 28
Edward II 20, 48
Edward III 31
Edward IV 20, 73
Edward, Prince of Wales 73, 85
Edwin, King of Northumbria 9, 20, 28
Egton Bridge 14, **56**
Elizabeth of York 31
Ellerton Priory 16, **79**
Ethelwald, King 68
Etty, William 38

Fairfax, Charles Gregory, 9th Viscount 35
Fairfax, Sir Thomas, 3rd Baron 20, 29, 66, 72
Fairfax family 11, 77
Falling Foss 18, **93-4**
Famous Connections 20
Farndale 18, **56**
Farrar, Reginald 66
Fauconberg, Earl of 52, 53
Fauconberg, Mary 53
Fawkes, Guy 20, 29, 34, 77
Fenton, Lavinia 91
Fenys, Dorothy & John 85
Festivals & Events 21
Feversham, Earl of 63
Filey 17, **57**
Flamborough Head 16, 17, **57**
Fountaine, Richard 70
Fountains Abbey *11*, 14, 15, 16, **57-8**
Fox, George 85
Fylingdales 9, 59

Gaping Gill Cavern 18, **66**
Gay, John 91
Gibbons, Grinling 52
Gilling East 15, 16, **58-9**
Goathland 16, 17, 18, *50* 59
Goldsmith, Peter 91
Gordale Scar 18, *54*, **71**
Gormire 18, **88**
Graham, Richard, Viscount Preston 76
Graham family 82
Grassington 17, 18, **59**
Great Ayton 17, **59-60**
Greathead, Henry 20, 80
Gresham, Sir Richard 57
Grey, Walter de, Archbishop 30, 34
Grinton 16, **60**
Guisborough 16, 19, **60**

Hackness 18, **60-1**
Hadrian 28
Halfdan 10
Harald Hardrada 10, 28
Hardrow Force 18, **63**
Harewood, Earl of 20
Harewood House 15, **61-2**
Harrogate 15, 17, 18, 19, **62**
Hartley, Marie 41, 62
Hawes 17, 18, **62-3**
Hawksmoor, Nicholas 48, 49
Haworth 17, **86**
Hayburn Wyke 18, **63**
Hearst, Randolph 58
Helmsley 14, 15, 16, 19, 52, **63**
Henry VII 31
Henry VIII 29, 38, 57
Herriot, James 20, 38, 63-4, 78, 89
Hilda, St 20, 93
Historic Houses 14-15
Hodgson, John 67
Hole of Horcum 18, **64**
Holtby, Winifred 48

Hood, Thomas 78
Hotels & Historic Inns 19
Hovingham 15, **64**
Howard, Catherine 38
Howard, Charles, Earl of Carlisle 13
Howard, Lord William 49
Howard family 48
How Stean Gorge 18, **71**
Hubberholme 14, *51*, **64**
Hudson, George 20, 29
Hume, Basil, Cardinal Archbishop of Westminster 20, 41
Hutchinson, Mary, *see* Wordsworth, Mary
Hutton, Captain Matthew 72
Hutton, Thomas 80
Hutton-le-Hole 17, **65**
Hyne, Charles John Cutliffe 67

I'anson, Frances 20, 80
Ilkley 8, 14, 16, 17, 18, 19, **65-6**
Ingilby, Joan 41, 62
Ingilby, Sir William Amcotts 81
Ingleborough Cave 18, **66**
Ingleton 18, 66

Jackson, John 69
James I (James VI of Scotland) 38, 81
Jenkins, Henry 45
Jervaulx Abbey 16, **66**
Johnson, Amy 46
Jones, Inigo 45
Jones, John Paul 57

Kauffmann, Angelica 61
Kearton, Cherry & Richard 20, 90
Keld 18, 19, **66**
Kent, Duchess of 20, 64, 75
Kent, William 37
Kilburn 16, 67
Kilnsey 15, 18, **67**
King, Robert & Nicholas 78
Kingsley, Charles 20, 41, 68, 71
Kiplin Hall 15, **45**
Kirk, Dr J. L. 36, 78
Kirkby Malham 14, **67-8**
Kirkbymoorside 14, **68**
Kirkham Priory 16, **68**
Kisdon Force 18, **66**
Knaresborough 12, 15, 16, 17, 18, 19, **68-9**
Knight, Dame Laura 20, 88

Lambert, John (Honest John) 20, 67
Lascelles family 61
Lastingham 14, **69-70**
Latimer, John Neville, Lord 53, 76
Lawrence of Arabia 20, 46
Leyburn 15, 17, **70**
Lilla, Thane 9
Lilla Howe 16, **59**

Lofthouse 18, **70-1**
Lord, Thomas 20, 89
Lytton, Lord 78

McNally, Leonard 80
Maiden Bower 16, 90
Maiden Castle 16, **60**
Malham 18, **71**
Mallyan Spout 17, **59**
Malton 8, 12, 14, 17, 19, **72**
Markenfield Hall 15, **82**
Marmion, Maude de 92
Marmion family 91-2
Marrick Priory 16, **79**
Marshall, John & William 78
Marston Moor 12, 16, 29, 72
Mary, Queen of Scots 11, 20, 45, 70, 82
Metcalf, John (Blind Jack) 69
Middleham 16, **73**
Monk, General 12
Moore, Temple 87
Morris, William 48, 76
Morrison, Walter 68, 71
Motoring Tours 24-5
Mount Grace Priory 16, 76
Mowbray, Robert de 89
Museums, Galleries & Visitor Centres 6, 16-17

Natural Features 17-18
Nature Reserves 18
Nesfield, W. A. 86
Neville, Anne 73
Neville, Charles, 6th Earl of Westmorland 68
Neville, Richard, Earl of Warwick 20, 73
Neville family 10, 73
Nevison, John 41
Newburgh Priory 14, 15, **53**
Newby Hall 14, 15, *50*, **73**
Newton Dale 18, **73-4**
Nidderdale 4-5, **74**
Northallerton 12, 19, **74**
North York Moors National Park 5, 75
North Yorkshire Moors Railway *50*, 75-6
Norton Conyers 15, **82**
Nun Monkton 14, **76**
Nunnington Hall 15, **76**

Osgodby Hall 15, **89**
Osmotherley 16, **76**
Oswy, King of Northumbria 9, 93
Otley 14, 17, 18, **76-7**

Parceval Hall 15, **41**
Parks, Gardens & Wildlife 15-16
Parr, Catherine 20, 53, 76, 87
Pately Bridge 16, 17, **77**
Paulinus, St, Bishop of York 9, 20, 28, 49
Pearson, J. L. 70
Percy, William de 64, 90

Percy family 10, 62
Philippa of Hainault 31
Pickering 14, 15, 16, 17, 19, **77-8**
Pilgrimage of Grace 11
Plompton Rocks 18, **62**
Postgate, Father Nicholas 56

Raistrick, Dr Arthur 70
Ranjitsinhji, Prince 59
Ravenscar 18, **78-9**
Redmayne, Sir Richard 62
Reeth 16, 17, **79**
Reynolds, Sir Joshua 72
Richard II 20, 69, 78
Richard III 20, 73, 85
Richmond 12, 14, 16, 17, **79-80**
Rievaulx Abbey 6, 16, **80**
Rievaulx Terrace & Temples 15, **81**
Ripley, Hugh 82
Ripley 14, 15, **81**
Ripon, 1st Marquis & Marchioness 58
Ripon 12, 15, 17, **81-2**
Roald, Constable of Richmond Castle 53
Robin Hood's Bay 47, 82
Roger, Archbishop of York 81
Rose, Joseph 61, 86
Roseberry Topping 17, 52, 60
Rupert of the Rhine, Prince 20, 29, 72

Saltwick Nab 18, **93**
Sandsend 15, **83**
Sansovino, Andrea 48
Scarborough 8, 12, 13, 15, 16, 17, **83-4**
Scoresby, Captain William (father and son) 20, 93
Scott, Rev. Alexander 49
Scott, Sir George Gilbert 63, 81
Scott, Sir Giles Gilbert 41
Scott, Sir Walter 20, 91
Scrope, John 45
Scrope, Sir Richard 44
Scrope family 11, 91
Semerwater 18, **84-5**
Septimius Severus 28
Settle 16, 17, 18, **85**
Sewerby Hall 15, **46**
Shandy Hall 15, **52**
Sheriff Hutton 16, **85**
Shipton, Mother 19, 20, 69
Simnel, Lambert 11
Sitwell family 20, 84
Skelton, Rev. Robert 70
Skipton 14, 15, 16, 17, **85-6**
Sledmere House 15, 18, **86-7**
Slingsby, Sir William 62
Smyth, Charles Piazzi 82
Snape 14, 15, **87**
Sport & Recreation 21-2
Staithes 18, **87-8**

Stamford Bridge, Battle of 28
Stanwick, Battle of 8
Stephenson, George 37, 75
Sterne, Lawrence 20, 52-3
Stoker, Bram 20, 93
Street, G. E. 87, 89
Strid *14*, 17, **44**
Studley Royal Park 15, 57, **58**
Stump Cross Caverns 17, **88**
Stuteville family 68
Sutcliffe, Frank Meadows 20, 93
Sutcliffe, Halliwell 70
Sutton Bank 18, **88-9**
Swaledale 4-5, **89**
Swastika Stone 65
Sykes, Sir Christopher 86, 87
Sykes, Sir Mark 87
Sykes, Sir Tatton 87
Sykes family 86

Taylor, Thomas 67
Thackeray, William Makepeace 20, 61
Thirsk, Robert 89
Thirsk 12, 14, 15, 17, 19, **89**
Thompson, Robert 41, 64, 67, 80, 92
Thornton, John 31
Thornton Dale 16, 17, 18 **89-90**
Thorpe Perrow Arboretum 15, **87**
Topcliffe, Thomas 90
Topcliffe, 14, 16, **90**
Tostig 28
Turner, J. M. W. 20, 77
Turpin, Dick 13, 20, 36
Tyrconnel, Lady 45

Vanbrugh, Sir John 13, 48
Verrio, Antonio 87
Vynes, F. Grantham 58
Vyner, Lady Mary 73

Wade's Causeway 49
Walker, John 92
Walks 22-4, 30-8
Walmsley, Leo 20, 82
Walter L'Espec 68
Weddell, William 73
Wensleydale 4-5, **91**
Wesley, John 76
West Tanfield *4-5*, 14, **91-2**
Wharfedale 4-5, **92**
Whitby 14, 16, 17, 18, **92-4**
White Scar Caves 18, **66**
Wilfrid, St 20, 81
Willance, William 80
William the Conqueror 94
William, Prince 31
Wilson, Leonard, Bishop of Birmingham 41
Woodforde-Finden, Amy 61
Wordsworth, William & Mary 20, 84

Worsley family 64
Wright, Austin 43
Wyatt, James 73, 82
Wyclif, John 20, 80
Wykeham Forest 84

York, Dukes of 29
York 6, 8, 9-10, 12, 13 **26-38;**
All Saints' Church 36;
Assembly Rooms 26, 29, 37; Bishopthorpe Palace 38; Castle Museum 27, 36, Churches 26; City Art Gallery 17, 38; Clifford's Tower 26, *28*, 36; Fairfax House 26, 35; Friargate Wax Museum 27, 36; Guildhall 26, 37; Heslington Hall 29; Historic Buildings 26-7; History 28-9; Holy Trinity Church 34; Hotels & Historic Inns 27; Jorvik Viking Centre 27, 35; King's Manor 26, 38; Mansion House 26, 37; Merchant Adventurers' Hall 26, 36-7; Merchant Taylors' Hall 26, 34; Minster 9, 26, 30-4, *39;* Moorlands Nature Reserve 27; Museum Gardens 27, 37; Museums, Galleries & Exhibition Centres 27; National Railway Museum 27, 36-7; Parks & Gardens 27; Rail Riders World 27, 37; Regimental Museum 27, 38; St Anthony's Hall 26, 34; St Mary's Abbey 27, *36-7*, 37-8; St Michaelle-Belfrey Church 34; St William's College 27, 34, *35;* Shambles 34; Treasurer's House 27, 34; University 29; Walls & gates 10, 29, *29*, 38, *39;* Yorkshire Museum 27, 37; Yorkshire Museum of Farming 27, 38; York Story 27
Yorkshire Dales National Park 4-5 **94**

Zucchi, Antonio 61, 73